THE

NEW ENGLAND COOK BOOK,

OR

YOUNG HOUSEKEEPER'S GUIDE:

BEING A
COLLECTION OF THE MOST VALUABLE RECEIPTS;
EMBRACING ALL THE
VARIOUS BRANCHES OF COOKERY,
AND
WRITTEN IN A MINUTE AND METHODICAL MANNER.

ALSO,
AN APPENDIX,
CONTAINING A COLLECTION OF MISCELLANEOUS RECEIPTS,
RELATIVE TO HOUSEWIFERY.

Kellscraft Studio
Chesterville, Maine

KELLSCRAFT STUDIO
2011

Original Publication Date:
1836.

ISBN: 978-1-105-40077-3

PREFACE

The writer deems that no apology need be offered for adding another to the long list of works on the truly interesting, if not noble science of gastronomy, provided she has accomplished the desirable object of producing a work that will commend itself to all persons of true taste; that is to say, those whose taste has not been vitiated by a mode of living contrary to her own. She has made that her aim, and although not an Ude or Kitchener, she does profess to have sufficient knowledge of the occult science, if properly imparted, to enlighten those not versed in culinary lore.

The utter inefficiency of most works of the kind, are well known to every experienced housekeeper, serving but to lead the uninitiated astray, who following implicitly the directions given have to lament in the language of that homely but not inapt proverb, that their cake is all dough. Among the few exceptions she would mention the Frugal Housewife by Mrs. Child, which is a very useful book, and fully answers its author's design; but that is limited as its name imports to the plainest cooking, and is not intended for those who can afford to consult their taste in preference to their purse. The writer of this short but she trusts comprehensive work, has endeavored to combine both economy, and that which would be agreeable to the palate, but she has never suffered the former to supersede the latter.

Although the mode of cooking is such as is generally

practiced by good notable Yankee housekeepers, yet the New England Cook Book is not so local but that it will answer like a modern almanac, without any material alteration for almost any meridian. It is intended for all classes of society and embracing both the plainest and richest cooking, joined to such minuteness of directions as to leave as little as possible to the judgment of the practitioner, proving to the unskilled quite a desideratum, while in the hands of the head of the culinary department, it will prevent that incessant running to and fro for directions, with which housekeepers' patience are too often tried. The experienced cook may smile at the simplicity and minuteness of some of the receipts, yet if she has witnessed as much good food spoiled by improper cooking as the writer of these receipts, she will not think she has been unnecessarily plain. In regard to the seasoning of food, it has been found impossible to give any exact rules, as so much depends on the quality of the food and seasoning.

The cook should be careful not to have the natural flavor of the food overpowered by the seasoning, and where a variety of spices are used, no one should predominate over the other.

Measuring has been adopted as far as practicable, in preference to weighing, on account of its being more convenient. As many people have not a set of measures, it has been thought best to use such utensils as every one has, viz. tumblers, tea cups, wine glasses, &c. but as they may be thought rather too indefinite by some, the exact quantity will here be stated; most tumblers are a good half pint measure, wine glasses usually hold half a gill, and table spoons the fifth of a gill; by tea cups are meant the old fashioned ones, which hold very little over a gill.

In conclusion the writer would give her sincere thanks, to those of her friends who have kindly furnished her with many of their choice and rare receipts, and to the public she would not add any thing more in its favor, being strongly impressed with the truth of the adage, that the proof of the pudding is in the eating.

CONTENTS.

1. Meat, ...1
2. Roast Beef, ...1
3. Beef Steak, ...2
4. Alamode Beef, ...2
5. Beef Liver, ...3
6. To Corn Beef, ...3
7. Mutton, ...4
8. Veal, ...5
9. Veal Cutlets, ...5
10. Calf's Head, ...5
11. Collops, ...6
12. Plaw, ...6
13. A Fillet of Veal, ...7
14. Lamb, ...7
15. Shoulder of Lamb Grilled, ...8
16. Lamb's Fry, ...8
17. Turkey, ...8
18. Goose, ...9
19. Chickens, ...9
20. Fricassee Chickens, ...10
21. Pigeons, ...11
22. Ducks, ...11
23. Baked Pig, ...11
24. Pressed Head, ...12
25. Souse, ...12
26. Tripe, ...13
27. Ham, ...13
28. Tongues, ...13
29. Curries, ...14
30. Curry Powder, ...14
31. Chicken Pie, ...14
32. Beef and Mutton Pie, ...15
33. Chicken and Veal Pot Pie, .15
34. To Frizzle Beef, ...16
35. Warmed over Meats, ...16
36. A Ragout of cold Veal, ...18
37. Drawn Butter, ...18
38. Burnt Butter, ...18
39. Roast Meat Gravy, ...18
40. Sauce for cold Meat,
    Fish or Salad, ...19
41. Wine Sauce for
    Venison or Mutton, ...19
42. Rice Sauce, ...19
43. Oyster Sauce, ...19
44. Liver Sauce for Fish, ...20
45. Lobster Sauce, ...20
46. Chicken Salad, ...20
47. Sauce for Turtle
    or Calf's Head, ...21
48. Apple Sauce, ...21
49. Pudding Sauce, ...21
50. Tomato Catsup, ...21
51. Mushroom Catsup, ...22
52. Essence of Celery, ...22
53. Soup Herb Spirit, ...22
54. Veal Soup, ...23
55. Black Soup, ...23
56. Calf's Head or
    mock Turtle Soup, ...24
57. Chicken or Turkey Soup, ..24
58. Oyster Soup, ...25
59. Pea Soup, ...25
60. To Bake Beans, ...25
61. Poached Eggs, ...26
62. To Boil Eggs, ...26
63. Omelet, ...26
64. Fresh Fish, ...27
65. Fresh Cod, ...28
66. Halibut, ...28
67. Striped and Sea Bass, ...28
68. Black Fish, ...28
69. Shad, ...28
70. Chowder, ...29
71. Stuffed and baked Fish, ...30
72. Salt Cod, ...30
73. Fish Cakes, ...30
74. Lobsters and Crabs, ...30
75. Scollops, ...31
76. Eels, ...31
77. Clams, ...32
78. Stew Oysters, ...32
79. To Fry Oysters, ...32
80. Oyster Pancakes, ...33
81. Oyster Pie, ...33
82. Scolloped Oysters, ...33
83. Vegetables.—Potatoes, ...33
84. Turnips, ...34

85. Beets,	....	34
86. Parsnips and Carrots,	....	34
87. Onions,	....	35
88. Artichokes,	....	35
89. Squashes,	....	35
90. Cabbage,	....	35
91. Asparagus,	....	36
92. Peas,	....	36
93. Beans,	....	36
94. Corn,	....	36
95. Greens,	....	37
96. Salads,	....	37
97. To Stew Mushrooms,	....	37
98. Egg Plant,	....	37
99. Celeriac,	....	38
100. Salsify or Vegetable Oyster,	...	38
101. Tomatoes,	....	38
102. Gumb,	....	39
103. Southern manner of Cooking Rice,	....	39
104. To Pickle Peppers,	....	39
105. Mangoes,	....	40
106. To Pickle Butternuts and Walnuts,	....	40
107. To Pickle Cabbage and Cauliflower,	....	41
108. To Pickle Onions,	....	41
109. To Pickle Artichokes,	....	41
110. To Pickle Cucumbers,	......	42
111. To Pickle Gherkins,	....	43
112. To Pickle Oysters,	....	43
113. To Pickle Mushrooms,	.....	43
114. Wheat Bread,	....	44
115. Sponge Bread,	....	45
116. Rye Bread,	....	45
117. Rice Bread,	....	46
118. French Rolls or Twists,	....	46
119. Yeast,	....	46
120. Yeast Cakes,	....	47
121. Biscuit,	....	48
122. Butter Milk Biscuit,	....	48
123. Hard Biscuit,	....	48
124. York Biscuit,	....	49
125. Rice Cakes,	....	49
126. Rice Ruffs,	....	49
127. Buck Wheat Cakes,	....	49
128. Economy Cakes,	....	50
129. Green Corn Cakes,	....	50
130. Corn Cake,	....	50
131. Indian Slap Jacks,	....	50
132. Johnny Cakes,	....	51
133. Hoe Cakes,	....	51
134. Muffins,	....	51
135. Flour Waffles,	....	52
136. Quick Waffles,	....	52
137. Rice Waffles,	....	52
138. Rice Wafers,	....	52
139. Observations respecting Sweet Cakes,	....	53
140. Gingerbread,	....	54
141. Soft Gingerbread,	....	54
142. Ginger Snaps,	....	55
143. Cider Cake,	....	55
144. Cookies,	....	55
145. New Year's Cookies,	......	56
146. Plain Tea Cakes,	....	56
147. Shrewsbury Cake,	....	56
148. Tunbridge Cake,	....	57
149. Jumbles,	....	57
150. Simbals,	....	57
151. Sugar Gingerbread,	....	57
152. Rusk,	....	58
153. Whigs,	....	58
154. Hot Cream Cakes,	....	58
155. Cross Buns,	....	59
156. Nut Cakes,	....	59
157. Crollers,	....	60
158. Molasses Dough Cake,	...	60
159. Sugar Dough Cake,	....	60
160. Measure Cake,	....	61
161. Cup Cake,	....	61
162. French Loaf,	....	61
163. Washington Cake,	....	62
164. Plain Cream Cake,	....	62
165. Rich Cream Cake,	....	62
166. Shelah or quick Loaf Cake,	...	62
167. Loaf Cake,	....	63
168. Rice Cake,	....	63
169. Diet Bread,	....	64
170. Scotch or Lemon Cake,	..	64
171. Pound Cake	....	64
172. Queen's or heart Cakes,	.	64

173. Jelly Cake, ...65
174. Raised Queen's Cake, ...65
175. Sponge Cake, ...66
176. Almond Sponge Cake, ...66
177. Black or Fruit Cake, ...66
178. Almond Cheese Cake, ...67
179. Maccaroons, ...68
180. Frosting for Cake, ...68
181. Cocoanut Cakes, ...69
182. Floating Island, ...69
183. Whip Syllabub, ...69
184. Blanc Mange, ...69
185. Rice flour Blanc mange, ...70
186. Ice Cream, ...70
187. Pastry, ...71
188. Puff Paste or
      Confectioner's Pastry, ...72
189. Apple Pie, ...72
190. Mince Pie, ...73
191. Peach Pie, ...74
192. Tart Pie, ...74
193. Rice Pie, ...75
194. Rhubarb or Persian
      Apple Pie, ...75
195. Cherry and
      Blackberry Pies, ...75
196. Grape Pie, ...75
197. Currant and
      Gooseberry Pies, ...76
198. Pumpkin Pie, ...76
199. Carrot Pie, ...76
200. Potatoe Pie, ...77
201. Marlborough Pie, ...77
202. Custard Pie, ...77
203. A Plain Custard Pie, ...78
204. Lemon Pie, ...78
205. Cocoanut Pie, ...78
206. Small Puffs, ...79
207. Boiled Custards, ...79
208. Almond Custards, ...79
209. Cold Custard
      or Rennet Pudding, ...80
210. Custard Pudding, ...80
211. Boiled Bread Pudding, ...80
212. A Plain Baked Bread
      Pudding, ...81

213. A Rich Bread Pudding, ...81
214. Flour Pudding, ...81
215. A Plain Rice Pudding, ...82
216. A Rich Rice Pudding, ...82
217. Rice Snow Balls, ...83
218. Baked Indian Pudding, ...83
219. Boiled Indian Pudding, ...83
220. Corn Pudding, ...84
221. Hasty Pudding, ...84
222. Fruit Pudding, ...84
223. Fritters, ...85
224. Apple Dumplings, ...85
225. Orange Pudding, ...85
226. Bird's Nest Pudding, ...86
227. Apple Custard Pudding, ..86
228. English Plum Pudding, ...87
229. Transparent Pudding, ...87
230. Lemon Syrup, ...87
231. Orange Syrup, ...88
232. Blackberry Syrup, ...88
233. Clarified Syrup for
      Sweet Meats, ...88
234. To Preserve Quinces, ...89
235. Quince Marmalade, ...90
236. To Preserve Pears, ...91
237. To Preserve Peaches, ...91
238. To Preserve Currants, ...92
239. To Preserve Barberries, ..92
240. To Preserve Ginger, ...92
241. To Preserve Apples, ...93
242. To Preserve Cymbelines
      or Mock Citron, ...93
243. To Preserve
      Watermelon Rinds, ...94
244. To Preserve Cherries, ...94
245. To Preserve Muskmelons, ...94
246. To Preserve Pine Apples, ...95
247. To Preserve Pumpkins, ...96
248. To Preserve Gages, ...96
249. To Preserve Strawberries, ...96
250. Blackberry and
      Raspberry Jam, ...97
251. Strawberry, Blackberry
      and Raspberry Jelly, ...97
252. Cranberry, Grape and
      Currant Jelly, ...97

253. Quince Jelly, ...98
254. Apple Jelly, ...98
255. Lemon Jelly,...................98
256. Calf's Foot Jelly, ...99
257. Coffee, ...100
258. To make Tea, ...101
259. Chocolate, ...101
260. Hop Beer, ...101
261. Spruce Beer, ...102
262. Spring Beer, ...102
263. Ginger Beer, ...103
264. A good Family Wine, ...103
265. Currant Wine, ...103
266. Raspberry Shrub, ...104
267. Noyeau, ...104
268. Spring Fruit Sherbet, ...105
269. Grape Wine, ...105
270. Smallage Cordial, ...105

MISCELLANEOUS RECEIPTS AND OBSERVATIONS
USEFUL TO YOUNG HOUSEKEEPERS.

1. To make Essence of Lemon, ...111
2. Essence of Ginger, ...111
3. Rose Water, ...111
4. Spice Brandy, ...112
5. Barley Water, ...112
6. Water Gruel, ...112
7. Wine Whey, ...112
8. Stomachic Tincture, ...113
9. Beef Tea, ...113
10. Carrageen or Irish Moss, ..113
11. Moss Blanc Mange, ...114
12. Elderberry Syrup, ...114
13. New Bread and Cake from old and rusked bread, ...115
14. To Preserve Cheese from Insects and Mould, ...115
15. To keep vegetables and herbs, ...116
16. To Preserve various kinds of Fruit over winter, .116
17. To extract Essences from various kinds of Flowers, ..118
18. Indelible Ink for marking linen, ...118
19. Perfume Bags, ...118
20. Lip Salve, ...119
21. Bread Seals, ...119
22. To Loosen the Glass Stopples of Decanters or Smelling Bottles when wedged in tight, ...120
23. Cement for broken China, Glass and Earthenware, ...120
24. Japanese Cement or Rice Glue, ...121
25. Cement for Alabaster, ...121
26. To extract fruit Stains, ...122
27. To extract Spots of paint from Silk, Woolen and Cotton Goods,...........122
28. To remove black stains on Scarlet Merinos or Broadcloths, ...122
29. To remove grease spots from Paper, Silk or Woolen, ...122
30. To extract stains from white Cotton goods and Colored Silks, ...123
31. Rules for washing Calicoes, ...124
32. Rules for washing Silks, ...124
33. Rules for washing woolens, ...125
34. Rules for washing white Cotton Clothes, ...126
35. To clean silk and woolen Shawls, ...127
36. To clean Silk Stockings, ...127
37. To clean Carpets, ...128
38. To clean feather Beds and Mattresses, ...128
39. To clean Light Kid Gloves, 129
40. To remove Ink or grease spots from Floors, ...129
41. To clean Mahogany and Marble Furniture, ...130
42. To clean stone hearths and stoves, ...130
43. To clean Brass, ...130
44. To cleanse Vials and Pie Plates. 131
45. Cautions relative to Brass and Copper, ...131
46. To keep Pickles and Sweet Meats, ...132
47. Starch, ...132
48. To temper new Ovens and Iron Ware, ...133
49. To temper Earthen Ware, 133

50. Preservatives against the ravages of Moths, ...133
51. To drive away various kinds of household vermin, ...133
52. To keep Meat in hot Weather, ...134
53. To Prevent polished Cutlery from rusting, ...134
54. To melt Fat for Shortening, ...134
55. To preserve Eggs fresh a year, ...136
56. To preserve Cream for long Voyages, ...136
57. Substitute for Milk and Cream in Tea or Coffee, ...136
58. To Cure Butter, ...136
59. To make salt Butter fresh, ...137
60. To take rankness from a small quantity of butter, .137
61. Windsor Soap, ...137
62. To make Bayberry or Myrtle Soap, ...137
63. Cold Soap, ...138

PRACTICAL COOKERY.

1. Meat.

To be in perfection meat should be kept several days, when the weather will admit of it. Beef and mutton should be kept at least a week in cold weather, and poultry three or four days. In summer meat should be kept in a cool airy place, away from the flies, and if there is any danger of its spoiling sprinkle a little salt over it. When meat is frozen it should be put in cold water and remain in it till the frost is entirely out, if there is any frost in it when put to the fire, it will be impossible to cook it well. Fresh meat should not be put into the pot until the water boils. When meat is too salt, soak it in lukewarm water for several hours, change the water before boiling it. Meat should boil gently with just water enough to cover it, and the side that is to go up on the table should be put down in the pot, as the scum that rises makes the meat look dark, it should be taken off as soon as it rises. The liquor in which all kinds of fresh meat is boiled, makes good soup.

2. Roast Beef.

The tender loin and first and second cuts of the rack are the best roasting pieces, the third and fourth cuts are good. The lower part of a rack of beef should be cut off as it prevents the meat from roasting thoroughly. When the beef is put to the fire to roast a little salt should be sprinkled on it, and the bony side turned towards the fire, when the ribs get well heated through, turn the meat, put it to a brisk fire and baste it frequently till done. If the meat is a thick piece allow fifteen minutes to each pound, to roast it in, if thin less time will be required.

3. Beef Steak.

The tender loin is the best piece for broiling, that from the shoulder clod or from the round is good and comes much cheaper. Beef before broiling if not very tender, should be laid on a board and pounded. Wash it in cold water, and broil it on a hot bed of coals, the quicker it is cooked without being burnt the better it is. Cut up about quarter of a pound of butter for 7 or 8 lbs. of beef, put the pieces into a platter and when the steak is done, lay it on the butter, pepper and salt it on both sides.

4. Alamode Beef.

The round of beef is the best piece to alamode. The shoulder clod is good and comes cheaper, it is also good stewed without any spices. For five lbs. of beef soak about a pound of bread in cold water, when soft drain off the water, mash the bread fine, put in a piece of butter, half the size of a hen's egg, together with half a tea spoonful of salt, the same quantity of mace, pepper, and cloves, also a couple of eggs and a table spoonful of flour, mix the whole well together, then cut gashes in the beef, and fill them with half of the dressing, put it in a bake pan with boiling water, enough to cover it. The bake pan lid should be just hot enough to scorch flour, put a few coals and ashes on the top, let it stew constantly for two hours, then place the reserved dressing on top of the meat, put in a piece of butter of the size of a hen's egg, heat the bake pan lid till hot enough to brown the dressing, stew it an hour and a half longer. When you have taken up the meat, if the gravy is not thick enough, mix a tea spoonful or two of flour with a little water, and stir it in, put in a couple of wine glasses of white wine, and a small piece of butter.

5. Beef Liver.

The best way to cook liver, is to pour boiling water on it, dip it in salt and water, then broil it till nearly done, with two or three slices of salt pork previously dipped in flour, cut up the meat and pork into strips about two inches long, lay the whole into a pan with a little water, salt and pepper, put in a little butter, stew it four or five minutes. It is more economical to fry or broil it, but it is not as nice.

6. To Corn Beef.

To every gallon of cold water, put a quart of rock salt, an oz. of salt petre, a quarter of a lb. of sugar and a couple of table spoonsful of blown salt. (Some people use molasses instead of sugar but it is not as good). No boiling is necessary, put your beef in the brine, as long as any salt remains at the bottom of the brine it is strong enough. Whenever any scum rises, the brine should be scalded, skimmed and more sugar, salt and salt petre put in. When a piece of beef is put in the brine a little salt should be added, and if the weather is warm cut gashes in the beef, and fill them with salt. Keep a heavy weight on the beef in order to keep it under the brine. The top of the weight is a good place to keep fresh meat from spoiling in hot weather. In very hot weather, it is difficult to corn beef in cold brine before it spoils, on this account it is a good plan to corn it in the pot, it is done in the following manner, to six or eight lbs. of beef put a tea cup of salt, sprinkle flour on the side that is to go up on the table and put it down in the pot, without any water in it, then turn in cold water enough to cover it, boil it two hours then fill up the pot and boil it an hour and a half longer.

7. Mutton.

The saddle, is the best part for roasting, the shoulder and leg are good roasted; but the latter is better boiled, with a piece of salt pork; a tea cup of rice, improves the looks of it. Before putting the mutton down to roast, rub a little butter on it, sprinkle on salt and pepper; cloves, and allspice improve it. Put a small piece of butter in the dripping pan, and baste it frequently, the bony side should be turned towards the fire first, and roasted. For boiling or roasting mutton, allow a quarter of an hour to each pound.

8. Veal.

The loin of veal is the best roasting

piece, the breast and rack are good roasting pieces, the breast makes a good pot pie. The leg is nice for frying, and when several slices have been cut off for cutlets the remainder is nice boiled with about half a pound of salt pork. Veal for roasting should be salted and peppered, and have a little butter rubbed on it, baste it frequently, and unless the meat is very fat put a small piece of butter in the dripping pan when the meat is put down to roast.

9. Veal Cutlets.

Fry three or four slices of pork, when brown take them up. Cut part of a leg of veal into slices about an inch thick and fry them in your pork fat, when brown on both sides take it up, stir about half a tea cup of clear water into the gravy, then mix a tea spoonful or two of flour with a little water and turn it in, soak a couple of slices of toasted bread in the gravy lay them on the bottom of a platter place your meat, and pork over the toast, then turn your gravy on the meat. Some people dip the veal into the white of an egg and roll it in pounded bread crumbs before cooking it. It takes nearly an hour to cook this dish.

10. Calf's Head.

Boil the head two hours together with the lights and feet, put in the liver when it has boiled an hour and twenty minutes, before the head is done, tie up the brains in a bag and boil them with it. When these are done take them up and mash them fine, season them with salt, pepper and butter, sweet herbs if you like, use them as the dressing for the head. Some people prefer part of the liver and the feet for dressing, they are prepared like the brains. The liquor that the calf's head is boiled in makes a nice soup seasoned in a plain way, like any other veal soup, or seasoned turtle fashion. The liquor should stand till the day after the head is boiled when the fat should be skimmed off.

11. Collops.

Cut part of a leg of veal into pieces three or four inches broad, sprinkle flour on them, and fry in butter till brown, then turn in water enough to cover the veal, when it boils take off the scum, put in two or three onions, a blade of mace, let it stew gently three quarters of an hour, put in a little salt, pepper and the juice of half a lemon. Take it up, pour the gravy over it. The gravy should be previously thickened with a little flour and water.

12. Plaw.

Boil a piece of lean veal till tender. Then take it up cut it into strips three or four inches long, put it back into the pot, with the liquor it was boiled in, and a couple of tea cups of rice to four lbs. of the veal, put in a piece of butter of the size of a hen's egg, season it with salt, pepper and sweet herbs, stew it gently till the water has nearly boiled away. A little curry powder in this converts it into a curry dish.

13. A Fillet of Veal.

Take a leg of veal, cut off the shank,

and cut gashes in the remainder. Make a dressing of bread soaked soft and mashed, season it with salt, pepper and sweet herbs, chop a little raw pork fine, and put it into the dressing, if you have not pork use a little butter. Fill the gashes in the meat with the dressing, put it in a bake pan with water enough to just cover it, put the remainder of the dressing on top of the meat. For six lbs. of veal, allow two hours steady baking. A leg of veal is nice prepared in this manner and roasted.

14. Lamb.

The fore and hind quarter of lamb are good roasting pieces. Sprinkle salt and pepper on the lamb and turn the bony side towards the fire first, if not fat, rub on a little butter and put a little in the dripping pan, baste it frequently. These pieces are good stuffed like a fillet of veal, and roasted, the leg is also good cooked in the same manner, but it is better boiled with a little pork or salt, allow fifteen minutes boiling to each lb. The breast of lamb is good roasted, broiled, or corned and boiled, it is also good made into a pot pie. The fore quarter with the ribs divided is good broiled, the bones of this as well as of all other kinds of meat when put down to broil should be put toward the fire, a little butter, pepper and salt should be put on it. Lamb is very apt to spoil in warm weather, if you wish to keep a leg several days, put it in brine, it should not be put in with pork, as fresh meat is apt to injure the pork.

15. Shoulder of Lamb Grilled.

The shoulder of lamb is good roasted or cooked in the following manner. Score it in chequers about an inch long, rub it over with a little butter and the yolk of an egg, then dip it into finely pounded bread crumbs, sprinkle on salt, pepper and sweet herbs, broil or roast it till of a light brown. This is good with plain gravy or sauce, made in the following manner, with half a pint of the gravy, (or the same quantity of drawn butter,) put a table spoonful of tomato catsup, the juice of half a lemon, a little salt and pepper.

16. Lamb's Fry.

The heart and sweet bread are nice fried plainly, or dipped into the white of an egg and fine bread crumbs, they should be fried in lard.

17. Turkey.

Take out the inwards and wash both the inside and outside of the turkey. Prepare a dressing of either boiled potatoes mashed fine or bread soaked in cold water, the water should be squeezed out of the bread, mash it fine, add a small piece of butter or pork chopped fine, put in pepper, salt, and sweet herbs if you like them, an egg mixed with the dressing makes it cut smoother. Fill the crop and body of the turkey with the dressing, sew it up, tie up the legs and wings rub on a little salt and butter. Roast it from two to three hours according to the size; twenty five minutes for every pound is a good rule. A turkey should be roasted slowly at first and basted frequently, the inwards of a turkey should be boiled till tender, and the liquor they are boiled in, used for the gravy, when you have taken up the inwards, mix a little flour and water smoothly together, and stir it into the skillet, put in a little of the drippings of the turkey, season it with salt and pepper, and sweet herbs if you like. Drawn butter is used for boiled turkey. A turkey for boiling should be dressed like one for roasting, tie it up in a cloth unless you boil rice in the pot with it, if you use rice, put in a tea cup two thirds full, a small piece of pork boiled with the turkey, improves it. If you wish to make a soup of the liquor in which the turkey is boiled, let it stand till the next day and then skim off the fat.

18. Goose.

If a goose is tender under the wing, and you can break the skin easily by running the head of a pin across the breast, there is no danger of its being tough. A goose should be dressed in the same manner, and roasted the same length of time, as a turkey.

19. Chickens.

Chickens for roasting or boiling, should have a dressing prepared like that for turkies. Half a tea cup full of rice boiled with the chickens, makes them look white, they will be less liable to break if the water is cold when they are put in to boil, a little pork boiled with the chickens improves them, if you do not boil any pork with them, put in a little salt. Chickens for broiling should be split, the inwards taken out, and the chicken washed inside and out, put the bony side down on the gridiron, and broil it very slowly till brown then turn it, when done take it up, salt, and butter it. About forty minutes is required to broil a common sized chicken. For roast chicken, boil the liver and gizzard by themselves and use the water for gravy, cut the inwards in slices, and put them in.

20. Fricassee Chickens.

The chickens should be jointed, the inwards taken out, and the chickens washed, put them in a stew pan with the skin side down, on each layer sprinkle salt and pepper; put in three or four slices of pork, just cover them with water, and let them stew slowly till tender. Then take them up, mix a tea spoonful of flour smoothly, with a little water, and stir it into the gravy, add a piece of butter of the size of a hen's egg, put the chickens back into the stew pan, let them stew slowly for four or five minutes. When you have taken up the chickens, put two or three slices of toast into the gravy, and when soaked soft lay it in a platter and lay the chickens on top, and turn the gravy upon it. If you wish to brown the chickens, reserve the pork and fry it by itself, when brown take it up and put in the chickens, (when they are stewed tender,) and let them fry till of a light brown.

21. Pigeons.

Take out the inwards and stuff them, with a dressing prepared like that for turkies, put them in the pot with the breast side down, the water should more than cover them, when nearly done put in a quarter of a lb. of butter to every dozen of pigeons, mix a little flour and water and stir into the gravy. When stewed tender, if you wish to brown them, take them up, and fry them in a little pork fat or butter, an hour before they are done, put on a heated bake pan lid. They are very good split open and stewed with a dressing made and warmed up separately with a little of the gravy. It takes about two hours to cook tender pigeons and three for tough ones. Tender pigeons are good stuffed and roasted. They should be buttered just before they are taken from the fire.

22. Ducks.

Are good stewed like pigeons, or roasted. Two or three onions in the dressing of wild ducks takes out the fishy taste. If ducks or any other fowls are slightly injured by being kept too long, dip them in weak saleratus and water before cooking them.

23. Baked Pig.

Take out the inwards, cut off the first joint of the feet and boil them till tender, take them up and take out the bones, chop them a little. Prepare a dressing of bread soaked and mashed fine, season it with salt, pepper, butter, and sweet herbs, if you like, fill the pig with the dressing, rub a little butter on the out side to prevent its blistering. If you wish to have it go on the table whole, put it into a long dripping pan, put in a little water, set it in a well heated oven, bake it from two hours and a half to three, according to the size. When done take out a little of the dressing, and mix it with the chopped inwards, and feet, put in a little butter pepper and salt, let the pig stand in the open air a few minutes before it goes on the table, in order to make it crispy.

24. Pressed Head.

Boil ears, forehead, and rind, (the cheek is good but is better corned and smoked), boil them till the meat will almost drop from the bones, take them up when cold, cut the meat in strips about an inch long and half an inch broad, warm it in a little of the liquor in which the meat was boiled, season it with pepper, salt, cloves, nutmeg and cinnamon, when hot take it up and put it in a strong bag, put a heavy weight upon it, and let it remain till perfectly cold.

25. Souse.

Take pig's ears and feet, clean them thoroughly, boil them till tender, take them out and when cold split them, lay them in a deep dish, pour on boiling vinegar strongly spiced with pepper corns, cloves and nutmeg, put in a little salt. When cold they are fit to cook. Fry them in lard. They will keep good pickled for four or five weeks.

26. Tripe.

After being scoured should be soaked in salt and water, seven or eight days, changing the water every other day. Then boil it till tender, which will take eight or ten hours. It is then fit for broiling, frying, or pickling. It is pickled like souse.

27. Ham.

A ham that weighs ten lbs. should be boiled four or five hours, if too salt the water should be changed. Before it goes on to the table take off the rind, put pepper or whole clove in the form of diamonds all over it. The Virginia way of curring Hams is the following, dissolve two oz. of salt petre, two tea spoonsful of sal eratus, for every 16 lbs. of ham, add molasses in the proportion of a gallon to a hogshead of brine. Make a salt pickle as strong as possible, put the above ingredients in it, then put the hams in, and let them remain for six weeks. Take them out and smoke them for three months. Hams cured in this way will keep good a long time and are very fine flavored.

28. Tongues.

Cut off the roots of the tongues, make a brine like that for curing beef, let the tongues remain in it for a week, then, smoke them eight or ten days. They require boiling four or five hours. The roots make very nice mince pies, but are not good smoked.

29. Curries.

Chickens, pigeons, mutton chops,

veal, lamb and lobsters, make good curries. The meat should be boiled till nearly tender, if made of fowls they should be jointed before they are boiled. Put a little butter in a stew pan, when melted put in the meat and cover it with part of the liquor it was boiled in, let it stew for ten or fifteen minutes. For 4 lbs. of meat, mix a table spoonful of curry powder, with one of flour, or a tea cup of boiled rice, put in a little water, and a table spoonful of melted butter, and half a tea spoonful of salt, turn the whole over the meat, and let it stew six or eight minutes.

30. Curry Powder.

Pound fine, one oz. of ginger, one of mustard, one of pepper three of coriander seed, the same quantity of turmeric, half an oz. of cardamums, quarter of an oz. of cayenne pepper, the same quantity of cinnamon and cummin seed. Pound the whole well together, sift and put them in a bottle.

31. Chicken Pie.

Joint the chickens, and boil them, till nearly tender in water just sufficient to cover them. Take them up and lay them in a dish, lined with pie crust, on each layer of the chickens, sprinkle pepper and salt, put in a little of the liquor that they were boiled in, three or four slices of pork and a small piece of butter, sprinkle flour over the whole. Cover it with a nice pie crust, ornament it with pastry cut in narrow strips. Bake it an hour and a quarter.

32. Beef and Mutton Pie.

Take meat that is tender, pound it out thin, and boil it ten minutes. Take it up, cut off the bony and gristly parts, season the meat highly with pepper and salt, butter it, and cut it in narrow strips. Line a deep dish, with piecrust, put in the meat, and to each layer, put a tea spoonful of tomato catsup, and a table spoonful of water, sprinkle flour over the whole, and cover it with piecrust, ornament it as you please with pastry. Cold roast, or boiled beef and mutton, cut in bits, and seasoned highly with salt and pepper, make a nice pie, put them in a dish, and turn a little melted butter over them, pour on water till you can just see it at the top.

33. Chicken and Veal Pot Pie.

Boil the meat until about half done, if chickens they should be jointed. Take up the meat, and put it in a pot with a layer of crust, to each layer of meat; have a layer of crust on the top, cover the whole with the liquor the meat was boiled in. Keep a tea kettle of boiling water, to turn in when the water boils away, (cold water makes the crust heavy.) If you wish to have it brown, heat a bake pan lid, and cover the pot while it is cooking, which takes about an hour. The crust for the pie is good, made like common pie crust, only very plain, roll it about an inch thick, cut it with a tumbler, into small cakes. Raised pie crust, is generally preferred to any other, it is made in the following manner. Rub together, three pints of flour one cup of butter, half a tea spoonful of salt, and then turn in a tea cup of yeast, and half a pint of water. Set it in a warm place to rise, when risen, (which will be in the course of ten or twelve hours, in cold weather,) roll it out, and cut it into small cakes. If it is not stiff enough to roll out, knead in a little flour, if too stiff, put in a little water. Potatoe pie crust is good, boil the potatoes, peel and mash them fine, put in a tea spoonful of salt, a piece of butter of the size of a hen's egg, and half a pint of milk, mix flour with it till of the right consistency to roll out, cut it into cakes, and put them with the meat. A very good way to make the crust, when you happen to have unbaked wheat bread; is to roll out the dough several times and spread butter on it each time, let it lay about half an hour, before you put it with the meat.

34. To Frizzle Beef.

Take tender smoked beef and shave it off thin, put it in a stew pan, with boiling water enough to cover it, let it stew ten or fifteen minutes; three or four minutes before it is done, thicken the water it is stewed in with a little flour, when taken up sprinkle on a little pepper. This makes a nice dish for breakfast, provided the beef is moist and tender.

35. Warmed over Meats.

Boiled or roasted veal makes a nice dish, chopped very fine, and warmed up with a little pepper, a small piece of butter, and a little water, if you have gravy, it is very good instead of the butter and water. A little nutmeg and the rind and juice of half a lemon improve it, the rind should be chopped very fine, (none of the white part should be used.) When well heated through, take it up and cut a couple of lemons in slices, and lay over it. Veal and fresh or salt beef, are all of them good, minced fine, with boiled potatoes, and warmed up with pepper, salt and gravy, if you have not gravy, use a little butter and water. Some people like boiled onions, or turnips, chopped fine, and mixed with the minced meat, instead of potatoes. Veal, lamb and mutton, are good cut in small strips, and warmed with boiled potatoes, cut in slices, and pepper, salt, and gravy. Roast beef and mutton, if not cooked too much, are nice cut in slices, and just scorched on a gridiron. Meat when warmed over, should only be on the fire just long enough to get heated well through, if on the fire long, most of the nourishment of the meat will be extracted, and it will be very indigestible. Cold fowls are nice jointed and warmed up, with a little water and salt, then take the fowls out of the water, put them in a frying pan, that has a little hot butter in it, and fry them, till of a light brown, they should have a little flour sprinkled over them before they are browned. Thicken the water with flour, that the fowls were warmed in, put a little butter in it, and turn it over the meat, when taken up.

36. A Ragout of Cold Veal.
Cut boiled or roasted veal, in nice

slices, flour and fry them in butter, till of a light brown. Then take them up and turn a little hot water into the butter they were fried in, mix a little flour with water and into the gravy, season it with salt, pepper, mace, and catsup, if you have any, and a little lemon juice. Put in the meat and stew it till very hot.

37. Drawn Butter.

Mix a couple of tea spoonsful of flour, gradually with a little water, stir it till free from lumps, thin it, and stir it into half a pint of boiling water, let it boil four or five minutes, then put in about a quarter of a lb. of butter, previously cut in small pieces, set it where it will melt gradually. If carefully mixed it will be free from lumps, if not strain it, before it is put on to the table. If the butter is to be eaten on fish, cut up several boiled eggs into it. A little curry powder sprinkled in it, will convert it into curry sauce.

38. Burnt Butter.

Put a couple of ounces of butter, in a frying pan, set it on the fire, when of a dark brown color, put in a table spoonful of vinegar, a little pepper and salt. This is nice for fish, or boiled eggs.

39. Roast Meat Gravy.

Meat when put down to roast, should have about a pint of water in the dripping pan. If you like your gravy very rich, skim off the top of the drippings to your meat, and use them, if you like it plain, stir up the drippings, strain them and put in a skillet and boil them. Mix a tea spoonful of flour, with a little cold water, and stir it into the gravy. Lamb and veal require a little butter in the gravy.

40. Sauce for cold Meat, Fish or Salad.

Mix the yolks of two eggs boiled soft, with a mustard spoonful of made mustard, a little salt and pepper, two table spoonsful of salad oil, or melted butter, when well mixed, put in three table spoonsful of vinegar. A table spoonful of tomato, or mushroom, catsup, improves it.

41. Wine Sauce for Venison or Mutton.

Warm half a pint of the drippings, or the liquor, the meat was boiled in. When it boils, mix a tea spoonful of scorched flour, with a little water, and stir it in, put in a little pepper, salt, and quarter of a tea spoonful of cloves, put in a table spoonful of currant jelly, and half a tumbler full of wine, just before you take it from the fire. Many people prefer melted currant jelly, to any other sauce for venison.

42. Rice Sauce.

Boil half a tea cup of rice, till soft, then stir in two table spoonsful of milk, a little salt, and a nutmeg, or mace, sweet herbs, a boiled onion, and strain it. This is a very nice accompaniment to game.

43. Oyster Sauce.

Take the juice of your oysters, and to a pint put a couple of sticks of mace, a little salt and pepper, put it on the fire, when it boils, mix two tea spoonsful of flour, with a little milk, and stir it in. When it has boiled two or three minutes, put in about half a pint of solid oysters, a piece of butter of the size of half an egg, when scalded through take them up.

44. Liver Sauce for Fish.

Boil the liver of the fish, then mash it fine, stir it into drawn butter, put in a little cayenne or black pepper, a couple of tea spoonsful of lemon juice, and a table spoonful of catsup.

45. Lobster Sauce.

Mash the yolks of two eggs, boiled soft, with the spawn of the lobster, and a tea spoonful of water, when rubbed smooth, put in a mustard spoonful of made mustard, two table spoonsful of salad oil, or melted butter, a little salt, pepper, and five table spoonsful of vinegar.

46. Chicken Salad.

Boil four eggs three minutes, take them out of the shell mash, and mix them, with a couple of table spoonsful, of olive oil, or melted butter, two thirds of a tumbler of vinegar, a tea spoonful of mixed mustard, half a tea spoonful of salt, quarter of a tea spoonful of pepper, and a little essence of celery, if you have any. Cut up a boiled chicken that weighs two or three pounds, into small strips, and turn the sauce over it.

47. Sauce for Turtle, or Calf's Head.

To half a pint of drawn butter, or

thickened beef gravy, put the juice of half a lemon, a little sage, basil, or sweet marjoram, a little cayenne pepper, and a wine glass of white wine, just before you take it up.

48. Apple Sauce.

Pare and quarter the apples, take out the cores, stew them in cider. When soft take them up, put in a piece of butter of the size of a walnut, to every quart of the sauce, sweeten it to your taste, with brown sugar. Another way which is very good, is to boil the apples, with a few quinces, in new cider, and molasses enough to sweeten them, till reduced to half the quantity. This kind of sauce will keep good for several months.

49. Pudding Sauce.

Mix a tea cup of butter, with two of nice brown sugar, when white, put in a wine glass of wine, or brandy, flavor it with nutmeg, essence of lemon or rosewater. If you wish to have it liquid make two thirds of a pint of thin starch, and stir it into the butter and sugar. If you wish to have it foam, put in a little cider. Cider instead of wine, or brandy, answers very well, for common pudding sauce.

50. Tomato Catsup.

Wipe the tomatoes, which should be perfectly ripe. Boil them till soft in a little water. Strain the whole through a sieve, season it highly, with salt, pepper, cloves, allspice and mace, then boil it fifteen minutes. Let it stand twenty four hours, then take off the watery part, bottle the remainder, seal it tight, and keep it in a cool place. Made in this way it will keep the year round. The catsup, should be stewed in tin, and the later in the season it is made, the less liable will it be to spoil.

51. Mushroom Catsup.

Put a layer of fresh mushrooms, in a deep dish, sprinkle a little salt over them, then put in another layer of mushrooms, and salt, and so on, till you get in all the mushrooms, let them stand several days, then mash them fine; to each quart, put a tea spoonful, of black pepper, put it in a stone jar tightly covered, set it in a pot of boiling water, boil it two hours, then strain it without squeezing the mushrooms. Boil the juice half an hour, skim it well, let it stand a few hours to settle, then turn it off carefully through a sieve, bottle, cork, and seal it tight, set it in a cool place.

52. Essence of Celery.

Steep half an oz. of bruised celery seed, in a quarter of a pint of brandy, for a fortnight. A few drops of this, will give a fine flavor to soup.

53. Soup Herb Spirit.

Those who like a variety of herbs, in soup, will find it very convenient, to have the following mixture. Take when in their prime, thyme, sweet marjoram, sweet basil, and summer savory, dry, pound, and sift them, steep them in brandy. The herb spirit will be fit for use, in the course of a fortnight.

54. Veal Soup.

A leg of veal, after enough has been cut off for cutlets, makes a soup nearly as good as calves head. Boil it with a cup two thirds full of rice, a pound and a half of pork, season it with salt, pepper, and sweet herbs, if you like, a little boiled celery cut in slices, or a little essence of celery improves it, parsly, carrot, and onions, boiled in the soup, are liked by some people. If you wish for balls in your soup, chop veal fine, mix it with a couple of eggs, a few bread crumbs, a small piece of butter, or raw pork chopped fine, put in salt and pepper, to your taste, or a little curry powder, boil them in the soup. Just before you take the soup up, put in a couple of slices of toast, cut into small pieces. The veal should be taken up before the soup is seasoned.

55. Black Soup.

The shank of beef, is the best part for soup, cold roast beef bones, and beef steak, make very good soup. Boil the shank four or five hours, in water enough to cover it. Half an hour before the soup goes on the table, take out the meat, thicken the soup with scorched flour mixed with cold water, season it with pepper, salt, nutmeg, and cloves, a little tomato catsup improves it, put in sweet herbs or herb spirit if you like. Some people boil onions in the soup, but as they are very disagreeable to many persons, it is better to boil them and put them in a dish by themselves. Take bread soaked soft, mash it well and put in a little of the boiled beef chopped fine, a couple of eggs, a very little flour, season it highly with salt, pepper, cloves, and mace, do it up in small balls and boil them in the soup fifteen minutes.

56. Calf's Head or mock Turtle Soup.

Boil the head till perfectly tender, then take it out, strain the liquor, and set it away till the next day, then skim off the grease. Cut up the meat, and put it in the liquor, together with the lights, (the brains should be reserved for the balls) warm it, and season it with salt, pepper, cloves, mace, and sweet herbs if you like and onions, let it stew gently for half an hour. Just before taking it up add half a pint of white wine. For the balls chop lean veal fine, with a small piece of raw salt pork, add the brains, and season it highly with salt, pepper, cloves, mace, and sweet herbs, or curry powder, make it up into balls, about the size of half a hen's egg, boil part in the soup, and fry the remainder, and put them in a dish by themselves.

57. Chicken or Turkey Soup.

The liquor that turkey or chicken is boiled in makes a good soup, with half a tea cup of rice, and a lb. of pork boiled in it. If you do not like it very fat, let it stand till the next day after the turkey is boiled, skim off the fat, season it with salt, pepper, and sweet herbs. If you like vegetables in soup, boil them by themselves, slice them up when done and put them in the turreen with toasted bread, cut in small pieces; or toasted crackers. When the soup is hot, turn it on them.

58. Oyster Soup.

Take a couple of quarts of oysters out of the liquor with a fork, strain the liquor, and if there are any shells in them rinse them off. To each quart put a pint of milk or water. Set them on the fire, when it begins to simmer skim it, mix three tea spoonsful of flour, with a little milk, stir it in when the oysters boil, when it boils again take it up and season it with salt, pepper, a table spoonful of tomato catsup, a table spoonful of vinegar and a small lump of butter; turn it on to a slice of toast cut in pieces.

59. Pea Soup.

To a quart of peas, put a quart of cold water soak them over night, in a warm place. Next day set them to boiling four or five hours, before they are to be eaten, put in a couple of lbs. of pork to two quarts of the peas, add in a little more water, if not likely to be sufficiently soft, put in a tea spoonful of saleratus half an hour before you take up the soup.

60. To Bake Beans.

Pick over the beans, wash, and put them in a pot with cold water enough to cover them, hang them over the fire where they will keep just lukewarm. When they begin to grow soft, stew them over a hot fire several minutes, with a heaping tea spoonful of saleratus. Then take them up with a skimmer, and put them in a baking pot, gash a lb. of pork and put it down in the pot so as to have the beans just cover it, pour in cold water till you can see it at the top. They will bake in a hot oven in the course of three hours; but they will be better to remain in it five or six. Beans are very good stewed, without being baked.

61. Poached Eggs.

Break your eggs into a dish and beat them to a foam. Then put them on a few coals, put in a small lump of butter, a little salt, let them cook very slowly, stirring them constantly till they become quite thick, then take them up, and turn them on buttered toast.

62. To Boil Eggs.

They should be put into boiling water, and if you wish to have them soft, three minutes is long enough to boil them, if you wish to have them hard, they should boil five minutes. Another way to boil them, is to break the shells and drop the eggs, into a frying pan of boiling water, let them boil three or four minutes. If you do not use the eggs, as a garnish, salt and butter them, when you take them up.

63. Omelet.

Beat your eggs to a froth, leaving out half the whites, put in a couple of ounces, of fine minced ham, corned beef or veal, when veal is used, a little salt will be requisite. Fry it in butter, till it begins to thicken. When it is brown on the underside, it is sufficiently cooked. If you wish to have it brown on the top, put a heated bake pan lid over it, as soon as it has set.

64. Fresh Fish.

Fresh fish for boiling, or broiling, are the best the day after they are caught. They should be cleaned, washed, and half a tea cup of salt, sprinkled on the inside of them, and a little pepper, if they are to be broiled. Set them in a cool place. When fresh fish are boiled, they should be put in a strainer, or sewed up in a cloth carefully; put them in cold water, with the backbone down; with eight or ten pounds of fish, boil half a tea cup of salt. Many people do not put their fish into the pot, until the water boils, but it is not a good plan, as the outside gets cooked too much, before the inside is cooked sufficiently. Fish for frying, should be wiped dry after being washed, and flour sprinkled on them. For five or six lbs. of fish, fry three or four slices of pork, when brown, take them up, and put in the fish, if the pork does not make sufficient fat, to fry the fish in, add a little lard. For good plain gravy, mix a tea spoonful or two of flour with a little water, and turn in, when you have taken up the fish; when well mixed, add a little butter and pepper, when it boils, turn it on to the fish. Boiled fish, should be served up with drawn butter, or liver sauce. For a garnish to boiled fish, boil several eggs five minutes, cool them in water, then take off the shells, and cut them in slices, and lay them round the fish; parsly and pepper grass, are also a pretty garnish for boiled fish. For broiling fish the gridiron should be greased with a little butter, the inside of the fish should be broiled first.

65. Fresh Cod,
Is good boiled, fried, baked, or made into a chowder. It is too dry a fish to broil.

66. Halibut,
Is nice cut in slices, and broiled or fried; the fins and the thick part, are good boiled.

67. Striped and Sea Bass,
Are good fried, boiled, broiled, baked or made into a chowder.

68. Black Fish.
Black fish are the best fried, or boiled, they will do to broil but are not so nice as cooked in any other way.

69. Shad.
Fresh shad are the best bloated and broiled; but they are good boiled or fried, the spawn and liver are nice fried in lard. Salt shad is good boiled, without any soaking, if liked quite salt, if not pour on scalding water, and let them soak in it, half an hour, then drain off the water, and boil them twenty minutes. Salt shad and mackerel for broiling, should be soaked twenty four hours, in cold water, the water should be changed several

times. To salt twenty five shad, mix one pound of sugar, a peck of rock salt, two quarts of fine salt, and quarter of a pound of salt petre. Put a layer of it at the bottom of the keg, then a layer of shad, with the skin side down, sprinkle on the mixed salt, sugar, and salt petre, and so on till you get in all the shad. Lay a heavy weight on the shad, to keep it under brine. If there is not brine enough in the course of a week, add a little more sugar, salt, and salt petre.

70. Chowder.

Fry three or four slices of pork until brown. Cut each of your fish into five or six slices, flour and put a layer of them in your pork fat, sprinkle on pepper and very little salt, cloves, and mace, if you like, lay on several crackers, previously soaked soft, in cold water, and several bits of your fried pork, this operation repeat, till you get in all your fish, then turn on nearly water enough to cover them, put on a heated bake pan lid. When the fish has stewed about twenty minutes, take them up, and mix a tea spoonful of flour, with a little water, and stir it into the gravy, add about an ounce of butter, and cloves. Half a pint of white wine, and the juice of half a lemon, or a tea cup of tomato catsup, improve it. Bass and Cod, make the best chowder. Some people like them made of clams, the hard part should be cut off.

71. Stuffed and Baked Fish.

Soak bread in cold water, till soft,

then squeeze out all the water, mash it and mix it with a piece of butter, of the size of a hen's egg, a little salt, pepper, cloves, and mace, a couple of raw eggs, makes the dressing cut smoother. Fill the fish with this dressing, and sew it up. Put a tea cup of water in a bake pan, and a small piece of butter, lay in the fish; bake it about an hour. Fresh cod, bass, and shad, are suitable fish for baking.

72. Salt Cod,

Should be soaked in lukewarm water, till the skin will come off easily. Scrape it, and change the water, and put it over a moderate fire, where it will keep warm without boiling, boiling hardens rather than softens it. It takes three hours to soak it soft. It should be cut into good square pieces, and served up with drawn butter. Cold codfish is good, minced up fine, with potatoes, and warmed up with butter, and a little water.

73. Fish Cakes.

Cold, boiled, salt, or fresh fish, are nice mixed up fine, with potatoes, a little butter put in, and moulded up, into small cakes, with the hand, fry them in pork fat, or butter.

74. Lobsters and Crabs.

Put them into boiling water, and boil them three quarters of an hour, if large, if not, half an hour will be long enough. Boil two thirds of a tea cup of salt, with four or five pounds of lobsters. When cold crack the shells, take out the meat.

Be careful to get out the blue vein, and what is called the lady, as they are very unhealthy. Lobsters are good cold, or warmed up, with a little vinegar, pepper, salt, and butter. A way of dressing them, which looks very prettily, is to pick out the spawn, and red chord, mash it fine, and rub it through the sieve, put in a little butter and salt, cut the lobsters into small squares, and warm it together with the spawn, over a moderate fire. When hot take it up, and garnish it with parsly. The chord and spawn when strained, are a handsome garnish for any kind of boiled fish.

75. Scollops.

Are nice fried, or boiled and pickled like oysters, for frying, they should be previously boiled, and taken out of the shells, and all but the hearts thrown away, as the rest is very unhealthy, dip the hearts, into flour, and fry them till brown in lard. The hearts are also good stewed with a little water, butter, pepper, and salt.

76. Eels.

If very large, are best, bloated and broiled, they should be bloated several hours before cooking them. If not very large fry them in pork fat; large eels are nice cut into small strips, and laid in a deep dish, with bits of salt pork and pepper, and baked for half an hour.

77. Clams.

Wash and boil them, until the shells

open, with just water enough to prevent their burning at the bottom of the pot. When the shells open, take the clams out of them, and warm them, with a little of the liquor, they were boiled in, and a little butter, pepper, and salt. Soak a slice of toasted bread, in the clam liquor, put it in the bottom of a dish and turn the clams on to it when hot. For clam pancakes, take some of the clam liquor, and mix with a little flour, to a pint of flour put two beaten eggs, and a little salt, fry them in lard. Very large long clams are nice taken out of the shell without boiling and broiled.

78. Stew Oysters.

Take the oysters out of the liquor with a fork, rinse the bits of shell from them, and strain the liquor, put the oysters in a stew pan, with the juice, when scalded through, take them up, turn them on buttered toast, salt, butter, and pepper them, to your taste, some cooks add a little catsup or lemon juice.

79. To Fry Oysters.

Take those that are large, dip them in eggs, and fine bread crumbs, fry them in lard, till of a light brown. They are a nice garnish for boiled or fried fish, if fried when first caught with a little salt, and pepper, sprinkled on them, will keep good several months, provided they are put into a bottle and corked tight, as soon as cooked. Whenever they are to be eaten, warm them with a little water.

80. Oyster Pancakes.

Mix the juice of the oysters, with

flour, in the proportion of a pint of liquor, to a pint of flour, if you have not juice enough, put in a little milk, or water, add a couple of eggs, and a little salt to each pint, fry them in lard.

81. Oyster Pie.

Line a deep dish with pie crust, fill it with dry pieces of bread; make a nice puff paste, and cover the dish with it, bake till of a light brown, either in a quick oven or bake pan, have the oysters just stewed, by the time the crust is done, take off the upper crust, and remove the pieces of bread, put in the oysters, season them with salt, pepper, and butter, a little catsup improves the pie, but is not essential, cover it with the crust.

82. Scolloped Oysters.

Pound crackers or rusked bread till fine, butter scolloped tins or shell, sprinkle on the crumbs, then put in a layer of oysters, a small lump of butter, a little pepper, salt, and juice of the oysters, put on another layer of crumbs, and oysters, and so on till the shells are filled, having the bread crumbs on top; bake them until a light brown.

83. Vegetables.—Potatoes.

The best way to cook potatoes, is to pare and put them in a pot, with just boiling water enough to prevent their burning, put in a little salt, and cover them up tight, let them stew till you can stick a fork through them easily. If there is any water in the pot turn it off, and put it back on the fire, and let the potatoes steam a few moments longer. The easiest way to cook them, is to put them in boiling water, with the skins on, they should boil constantly till done, if you wish to have them mealy; they are more mealy, to have the water turned off, as soon as you can stick a fork through them easily, and put in a warm place, where they will steam, the lid should be off. Cold, mashed, or whole potatoes are nice cut in slices, and fried in lard or butter. Sweet potatoes are the best baked. Most potatoes will boil sufficiently in half an hour, new Irish potatoes will boil in less time.

84. Turnips.

White turnips require about as much boiling, as potatoes. When tender take them up, peel and mash them, season them with a little salt and butter. Yellow turnips require about two hours boiling, if very large, they should be split in two.

85. Beets.

Beets should not be cut, or scraped before they are boiled. In summer they will boil in an hour, in winter it takes three hours to boil them tender. Boiled beets cut in slices, and put in vinegar, for several days, are nice.

86. Parsnips and Carrots.

The best way to cook them, is to scrape and split them in two, put them in a stew pan with the flat side down, pour on boiling water enough to cover them, when done take them up, and butter them. Many people boil parsnips whole, but it is not a good plan, as the outside gets done too much, before the inside is cooked sufficiently.

87. Onions.

Peel and put them in boiling milk, water will do to boil them in but is not as good, when done take them up salt them, and turn a little melted butter, over them.

88. Artichokes.

Scrape and put them in boiling water with a table spoonful of salt, to a couple of dozen, when boiled tender (which will be in about two hours) take them up and butter them.

89. Squashes.

If very young boil them whole, if not they should be pared quartered and the seeds taken out, boil them till very tender, then take them up, put them in a cloth, and press out the water, mash them in a dish, salt and butter them to your taste.

90. Cabbage.

Take off the loose leaves, cut the stalky part in quarters, to the heart of the cabbage. Boil it an hour, if not boiled with corn beef put a little salt in the pot. Cauliflowers will boil tender in fifteen or twenty minutes.

91. Asparagus.

The tough part should be cut in thin

slices, and boiled eight or ten minutes, before the other part is put in, lay the remainder compactly together, tie it in small bundles and boil it from fifteen to twenty minutes, according to its age. Take it up when tender, with a skimmer lay it on buttered toast, in a deep dish, sprinkle a little salt on it, melt a little butter, and turn over it.

92. Peas.

Shell and boil them, from fifteen to thirty minutes, according to their age, and kind, if very old a tea spoonful of saleratus boiled with them, makes them better and more healthy. When tender take them up salt and butter them to your taste.

93. Beans.

String beans, should have the strings carefully taken off and if old, the edges should be cut off; if the beans are old put saleratus in the pot, in the proportion of half a tea spoonful of saleratus, to a peck of beans it should be put in before the beans. Boil them from twenty five to thirty minutes, salt and butter them when you take them up. Beans and all other summer vegetables, should not be picked longer than one day before being cooked; the fresher green vegetables are the better they are and more healthy.

94. Corn,

Should be put in boiling water with a little salt, and boiled from ten to twenty minutes, according to its age. It is much sweeter to be boiled on the cob.

95. Greens.

White mustard, spinach and the leaves and roots of very small beets, are the best greens. Boil them with a little salt and saleratus in the water.

96. Salads,

Should be fresh, and put in cold water, for half an hour before they are eaten. Cucumbers, to be healthy, should not be picked longer than a day before they are eaten, they should be kept in cold water, and fifteen or twenty minutes before they are eaten, pare and slice them, into fresh cold water.

97. To Stew Mushrooms.

Peel and put them in a sauce pan, with just enough water, to prevent their burning to the bottom of the pan. Put in a little salt, and shake them occasionally. When they have stewed about twenty minutes, put in a little butter, pepper, and salt; a little wine and cloves improve them. They should be stewed very slowly, and taken up as soon as seasoned, turn them on buttered toast.

98. Egg Plant,

Should be cut in slices, about half an inch thick, between every slice sprinkle a little salt, let them lay two hours before cooking, then scrape off the salt and fry them till brown in lard.

99. Celeriac.

This is an excellent vegetable, but it is but little known. The stalks of it, can hardly be distinguished from celery, and it is much easier cultivated. The roots are nice boiled tender, and cut in thin slices and put in soup, or meat pie, or cooked in the following manner, and eaten with meat. Scrape and cut them in slices, and boil them, till perfectly tender, then take them up sprinkle on a little salt and stew them in a little milk four or five minutes, turn them into a dish, and put in a little butter.

100. Salsify or Vegetable Oyster.

The best way too cook it, is to cut it in slices, and dip it into an egg and fine bread crumbs, fry it in lard. It is very good boiled, and then stewed a few moments in milk, and a little butter put on it, or cut in slices, and fried in butter, made like that for oyster pancakes, substituting milk for the juice of the oyster.

101. Tomatoes,

If very ripe will skin easily, if not pour on scalding water, and let them remain in it four or five minutes. Peel and put them in a stew pan with a table spoonful of water if not very juicy, if so no water will be required, put in a little salt, and stew them in tin, for half an hour, when done turn them into a dish with buttered toast. Another way of cooking them, which is considered very nice by epicures, is to put them in a deep dish, with powdered bread crumbs, or crackers, a layer of each alternately, sprinkle salt, and pepper, on each layer, and put on small bits of butter, over each layer, some people like a little nutmeg and sugar. Have a layer of bread crumbs on the top, and bake it, in a bake pan three quarters of an hour.

102. Gumb.

Take an equal quantity of young tender okra chopped fine, and ripe tomatoes skinned, an onion shredded fine, a small lump of butter, a little salt and pepper, put the whole in a stew pan, with a table spoonful of water, and stew it till tender.

103. Southern Manner of Cooking Rice.

Pick over the rice, and wash it in cold water, put it in three quarts of boiling water with half a tea spoonful of salt, to a pint of the rice. Boil it seventeen minutes, then turn off the water very close, put it over a moderate fire with the lid of the pot off, let it steam fifteen minutes. Rice boiled in this manner is superior to any other; but care must be taken to be exact in the time of boiling and steaming, as a few moments variation makes a great deal of difference with it, the water should boil when it is put in the pot, and not allowed to stop boiling till done. The water that the rice is cooked in makes nice starch if boiled a few moments by itself.

104. To Pickle Peppers.

If you do not like them fiery, take out the seeds, they should be taken out carefully with a penknife, so as not to mangle the pepper. Soak them in salt and water, eight or nine days, change the water each day, and keep them in a warm place. If you like them stuffed, put in cinnamon, cloves, mace, and nasturtions, lay them in cold spiced vinegar. Tomatoes when very small, and green, are good pickled with the peppers.

105. Mangoes.

Procure muskmelons as late in the season as possible, and those that are very green; if pickled early, they are apt to spoil. Take out the seeds, and soak them in salt and water, three or four days. Then take them out of the water, sprinkle powdered cloves, and nutmeg, round on the inside of the melon, fill them with strips of horseradish, cinnamon, small string beans, or flag root, nasturtion, and radish tops, fill the crevices, with American mustard seed; put on the covers, and sew each one up in a bag. Lay the melons in a stone jar, with the side that the covers are on up; turn on scalding hot vinegar, with alum, pepper corns, and salt in it. Pickled barberries are a pretty garnish for them.

106. To Pickle Butternuts and Walnuts.

The nuts for pickling should be picked as early as the first of July unless the season is very backward, if a pin will go through them easily, they are in a right state for pickling. Soak them in salt and water, a week, then drain, and scrape or rub them, with a cloth, sprinkle them with ground cloves, and pour on boiling vinegar, spiced with cloves, pepper corns, allspice, and mace, add a little salt. They will be fit to eat in the course of a fortnight, or three weeks. The vinegar they are pickled in, makes a nice catsup, if boiled down to half the quantity, and a little more spice added.

107. To Pickle Cabbage, and Cauliflower.

Purple cabbages are the best for pickling. Pull off the loose leaves and quarter them, sprinkle salt on the flat side of each one, let them lay several days, then rinse off the salt and drain them; sprinkle on powdered cloves, mace, salt, and pour on scalding vinegar, with a few peppers in it, alum and pepper corns. Cauliflowers are pickled in the same manner as the cabbages. They will be fit to eat in the course of a fortnight, after being pickled.

108. To Pickle Onions.

Peel and boil them, in milk and water, a few minutes. Put cloves, cinnamon, mace, and salt, in vinegar, and heat the vinegar scalding hot in brass. Take the onions out of the milk and water, drain them, then turn on the vinegar scalding hot, with two ounces of alum to each pailful of vinegar. Cover them tight until cold.

109. To Pickle Artichokes.

Soak the artichokes in salt and water, a week, then drain and rub them, till you get all the skin off, turn boiling vinegar on them, spiced with pepper corns and mace, add salt and alum. Let them remain a week, then turn off the vinegar, scald it, and turn it back, while hot on to the artichokes. Continue to scald the vinegar, at intervals of a week or ten days, until the vinegar appears to have entered the artichokes.

110. To Pickle Cucumbers.

Pour boiling water on them, when first picked; and let them lay in it eight or ten hours, then put them in cold vinegar, with alum and salt, in the proportion of quarter of a pound of the first, and a pint of the last, to every half barrel of pickles. When you have done picking your cucumbers for pickling, turn the vinegar from them, boil and skim it till clear, throw in the cucumbers, and let them boil a few moments, then put them in fresh cold vinegar, with salt and alum; a few peppers improve them. Whenever any scum rises on any kind of pickles turn off the vinegar, scald and skim it, turn it back when cold on the pickles. Pickles of all kinds should be stirred up occasionally, and if there are any soft ones among them, they should be thrown away, and the vinegar scalded; if very weak, it should be thrown away and fresh added. The vinegar when scalded, should not be allowed to cool in brass. Another method of pickling cucumbers, which is very good, is to put them in salt and water, as you pick them, change the water once in three days; when you have done picking your cucumbers, take them out of the salt and water, and put

them in cold vinegar, with alum, salt, and
pepper corns in it.

111. To Pickle Gherkins.

Put them in strong brine, keep them
in a warm place, when they turn yellow,
drain off the brine, and turn hot vinegar
on them, let them remain in it near the
fire till they turn green, turn off the
vinegar, and pour on fresh hot vinegar,
spiced with pepper corns, mace, cloves,
and cinnamon; add salt and alum in the
same proportions as for cucumbers.
These, as well as all other pickles,
should not be kept in glazed earthen
jars.

112. Oysters.

Take the oysters from the liquor,
strain and boil it, then put in the oysters,
let them boil one minute, take them out,
and to the liquor, put a few pepper
corns, cloves, a little mace, and the
same quantity of vinegar as oyster juice,
boil it fifteen minutes; when cold turn it
on to the oysters. Bottle and cork them
tight.

113. Mushrooms.

Peel and stew them, with just water
enough, to prevent their sticking to the
bottom of the stew pan, shake them
occasionally, to prevent their burning.
When tender take them up, and put
them in scalding vinegar, spiced with
mace, cloves, and pepper corns, add a
little salt, bottle and cork them up.

114. Wheat Bread.

For six common sized loaves of bread, take three pints of boiling water, and mix with five quarts of flour; when thoroughly mixed, add three pints of cold water, stir it till the whole of the dough is equally cold; when lukewarm stir in half a pint of yeast, a table spoonful of salt, knead in flour till stiff enough to mould up, cover it over and if the weather is cold set it near the fire to rise. To ascertain when it is risen, cut it through the middle with a knife, and if full of small holes like a sponge, it is sufficiently light. If the dough gets sour before you are ready to bake it, dissolve two or more tea spoonsful of saleratus (according to the acidity of it,) in a cup of water, and strain it on the dough, work it in well, mould it up, slash it on the sides, to prevent its cracking when baked, put it in buttered pans, and let it stand ten or twelve minutes before you bake it; if you like it quite brown let it stand in the oven an hour and a half. If the wheat is grown, use all boiling water, and let it stand till cool before putting in the yeast. Some people, have an idea that it kills the life of the flour, to scald it, but it is a mistake, it makes it much sweeter, and prevents its moulding soon in warm weather; bread made in this manner is very nearly as good as that which is wet with milk. Care must be taken, not to put in the yeast when the dough is hot, as it will scald it and prevent its rising. Bread is much better in the winter, for being made several days before it is baked, it should be kept in a cool place, and a little flour knead in every day. Most ovens require heating an hour and a half for bread, some will heat sufficiently in an hour, a brisk fire should be kept up, the doors in the room should be kept shut in cold weather. Pine, and ash, or birch mixed, are the best wood for heating an oven. To ascertain if your oven is of the right temperature, when cleared throw in a little flour, if it browns in the course of a minute, it is hot enough, if it turns black wait several minutes before you put in your things, if not hot enough, set in a furnace of live coals, after you have put your things in.

115. Sponge Bread.

For four loaves of bread, take three quarts of boiling water and turn it into three quarts of flour. When lukewarm put in a cup of yeast, a table spoonful of salt, set it in a warm place to rise, when light knead in flour till stiff enough to mould up, then let it stand till risen again, before moulding it up.

116. Rye Bread.

Wet up the rye flour with lukewarm milk, if you have it; if not water will do, and the same proportion of yeast as for wheat flour; put in a small piece of butter and a little salt. It should not be kneaded as stiff as wheat flour, as it will be hard when baked; let it stand in the pans, after it is moulded up, half an hour. Brown Bread is made by mixing, Indian meal and Rye flour. The Indian meal should be scalded; when cool, put in the rest of the ingredients, in the same

proportion as for plain rye bread. Bake it
between two and three hours.

117. Rice Bread.

Boil a pint of rice till soft, then mix it
with two quarts of rice flour, a tea cup of
yeast, two tea spoonsful of salt, and milk
enough to render it of the consistency of
rye bread. When light bake it in small
loaves.

118. French Rolls, or Twists.

Turn a pint of lukewarm milk, into a
pint of flour, mix them well together, then
turn in a small tea cup of yeast, two tea
spoonsful of salt, and flour enough to
make a thick batter. Set it in a warm
place to rise. When light, put in a piece
of butter of the size of a hen's egg, and
half a tea cup of lukewarm water, the
butter should be melted before it is put
in; knead in flour until stiff enough to roll
out. Let it stand till risen again, then roll
it out, about half an inch thick, cut it into
narrow strips, braid and twist them a
little, as you braid them. Lay them on flat
buttered tins, let them remain from
twenty to thirty minutes, then bake them
slowly.

119. Yeast.

Boil a small handful of hops, in two
quarts of water, when all the strength is
obtained from them, strain the liquor,
and put it back on the fire, take a little of
it, and mix smoothly with a couple of
table spoonsful of flour, mix it with the
boiling liquor, when it has boiled five or
six minutes, take it from the fire, and

when lukewarm, add a tea cup of yeast, keep it in a warm place till risen, then stir in a table spoonful of salt, turn it into a jar, and cover it up tight. Some people keep yeast in bottles but they are very apt to burst. Yeast made in this manner, will keep a fortnight in the warmest weather. If your yeast appears to be sour, put a little sal eratus in just before you put it into your bread; if it does not foam well, it is too stale to use. Another method of raising bread, which is very good, is to leave about half a pound of dough, from one week's baking to another. It should be rolled out thin and dried in the sun, about two hours before you wish to bake your bread, turn a quart of warm water to it, and set it near the fire till light, which will be in the course of an hour, then scald your dough, and when lukewarm, stir in the yeast; it will raise the bread in the course of an hour. This can only be used two or three times, without having fresh yeast put to it.

120. Yeast Cakes.

Stir into a pint of yeast, a table spoonful of salt, and Indian meal sufficient to enable you to roll it out. When rolled thin, cut it into cakes with a tumbler, and dry them in the wind; in hot weather, care must be taken to keep them from the sun, or they will ferment; when perfectly dry, tie them up in a bag, and keep them in a cool dry place. To raise four or five loaves of bread, take one of these cakes, and put it in half a pint of warm water, set it near the fire to

rise, when light use it to raise your
dough.

121. Biscuit.

Melt a cup of butter, and mix it with
half a pint of lukewarm milk; if you have
not milk, water will do, add a tea cup of
yeast, two tea spoonsful of salt, and
flour to render it sufficiently stiff to roll
out. Set it in a warm place, when light,
roll it out about an inch thick, cut it with a
tumbler into cakes and let them stand
half an hour before baking them.

122. Butter Milk Biscuit.

Dissolve a couple of tea spoonsful of
saleratus, in a tea cup of milk, sour is
the best. Mix it with a pint of buttermilk,
three tea spoonsful of salt; a little cream
improves it; knead in flour till stiff enough
to roll out. Mould it into small cakes, and
bake them directly.

123. Hard Biscuit.

Weigh out four pounds of sifted
flour; take out about a quarter of a
pound of it, rub the remainder with four
ounces of butter, two tea spoonsful of
salt, and four eggs. Wet up the whole
with milk, pound it out flat with a rolling
pin, sprinkle a little of the reserved flour
over it lightly, roll it up and pound it out
thin again, sprinkle on more of the flour,
roll it up, this operation continue to
repeat, until you get in all the reserved
flour. Then mould it up into small cakes,
lay them on flat buttered tins, flatten and
cover them, with a damp cloth as you lay
them on the tins, to prevent their drying

too fast. Bake them in a quick oven.

124. York Biscuit.

Rub together six ounces of butter, two pounds and three quarters of flour, dissolve a couple of tea spoonsful of saleratus in a little milk, and mix it with the flour, add a tea spoonful of salt, and milk sufficient to enable you to roll it out. Pound it out thin and cut it into cakes, bake them till a light brown.

125. Rice Cakes.

Mix a pint of soft boiled rice, with a pint of milk, or water, a tea spoonful of salt and a couple of beaten eggs. Stir in rice or wheat flour, till of the right consistency to roll out. Cut them into cakes and bake them.

126. Rice Ruffs.

To a pint of rice flour, put a pint of boiling water, a tea spoonful of salt, and four eggs, beaten to a froth. Drop this mixture into boiling fat, by large spoonsful.

127. Buck Wheat Cakes.

Mix a quart of buck wheat flour, with a pint and a half of warm milk, (water will do but is not quite as good) and a tea cup of yeast, then set it in a warm place to rise. When light (which will be in the course of ten or twelve hours,) add a tea spoonful of salt, if sour the same quantity of saleratus, dissolved in milk, and strained, thin them with a little milk. Fry them in just fat enough to prevent their sticking to the griddle or pan. Salt pork rinds, beef fat, or lard, are good to fry them in.

128. Economy Cakes.

Soak dry pieces of bread in water, till soft enough to mash fine, squeeze out all the water, and to three pints of the bread pulp, put a couple of table spoonsful of flour, one beaten egg, half a tea spoonful of salt, the same quantity of saleratus, dissolved in a cup of milk and strained. If not thin enough stir in a little more milk. Cook them in the same manner as buck wheat cakes.

129. Green Corn Cakes.

Mix a pint of grated green corn, with three table spoonsful of milk, a tea cup of flour, half a cup of melted butter, one egg, a tea spoonful of salt, half a tea spoonful of pepper. Drop this mixture by the spoonful into hot butter, and fry it eight or ten minutes. These cakes are nice served up with meat for dinner.

130. Corn Cake.

To a quart of milk put three beaten eggs, a tea spoonful of salt, mix it with sifted Indian meal enough to make a thin batter. Bake it in a bake pan about one hour. Buttermilk or sour milk with a tea spoonful of saleratus, is better to mix with the Indian meal, than sweet milk and eggs.

131. Indian Slap Jacks.

Mix a quart of milk with a pint of Indian meal, four table spoonsful of flour, three beaten eggs, a tea spoonful of salt. A table spoonful of molasses or a little stewed pumpkin is thought by many people to improve them. Fry them in lard. Another way which is very good, is to scald a quart of Indian meal and half a pint of wheat flour with milk, (water will do but is not as good) stir in a small tea cup of yeast and set them in a warm place to rise. When light fry them, in just fat enough to prevent their sticking to the griddle.

132. Johnny Cakes.
Scald sifted Indian meal, put in a little salt, mould it with the hand into cakes, of the size of biscuit. In order to mould them up, considerable flour must be rubbed on the hands. Fry them in fat enough to cover them. When cooked split and butter them.

133. Hoe Cakes.
Stir up Indian meal, with cold water sufficient to make a batter, of the consistency of buck wheat cakes, add a tea spoonful of salt, a table spoonful of melted butter. Butter your bakepan and turn this mixture into it and bake it about an hour. Indian meal wet up in this manner is good fried.

134. Muffins.
Mix a pint of lukewarm milk, with the same quantity of flour, a tea spoonful of salt, a piece of butter, of the size of a hen's egg. When light beat a couple of eggs and put in; butter muffin rings, and put them in a buttered pie pan, turn in the mixture and bake them till of a light

brown.

135. Flour Waffles.

Gradually turn a quart of milk or water on to a quart of flour, stirring it well as you turn it in, so that it may not be lumpy, add a tea cup of yeast, a tea spoonful of salt, a table spoonful of melted butter, a couple of eggs, improve them, but they can be dispensed with very well. When light bake them in waffle irons, well heated and greased with lard, before each one is poured in. Bake them on hot coals; when they have been on the fire about two minutes, turn the irons, and let them brown on the other side.

136. Quick Waffles.

Into a quart of flour stir slowly a quart of milk or water, beat five eggs and put in, together with a tea spoonful of salt and a table spoonful of melted butter. They are cooked in the same manner as other waffles. A quarter of a pound of sugar, stirred into the mixture improves it.

137. Rice Waffles.

Mix a quart of milk with a tea cup of boiled rice, and a pint and a half of rice or wheat flour. Beat three eggs to a froth, and stir in, together with a tea spoonful of salt.

138. Rice Wafers.

Rub a pound of rice flour, with quarter of a pound of butter, put in a little salt, a wine glass of wine, two eggs, and milk sufficient to enable you to roll them out. When rolled thin, cut them with a wine glass into small cakes and bake them.

139. Observations respecting Sweet Cakes.

If you wish your cake to be good, it must be made of nice materials. The butter, eggs, and flour should not be stale, and the sugar should be dry, and of a light color. Brown sugar answers for most kinds of cakes, if rolled free from lumps, and stirred with the butter, until it is a very light color. The flour should be sifted and if damp, it should be dried perfectly, or it will make the cake heavy. Where sifted flour for cake is measured, it should be shaken down in the measure to be accurate; if there is not flour enough in cake, it will not be light. The eggs should be beaten to a froth, on a shallow plate, and for very nice cake the whites and yolks, should be beaten separately. Where saleratus is used, it should be thoroughly dissolved and strained. Raisins for cake, should have the seeds taken out, and Zante currants should be carefully washed and rubbed in a cloth, to get out the sticks; they should be perfectly dried before they are put into the cake. All kinds of cake that has not yeast in it, should be stirred till it goes into the oven. It should not be moved while in the oven, if it can be avoided. The quicker most kinds of cake are baked, without burning, the better they will be. It is impossible to give any exact rules as to the time for baking cake, as so much depends on the heat of the oven; it should be narrowly watched and if likely to burn covered with a thick paper. To ascertain when rich cake is sufficiently baked, stick a clean broom splinter through the thickest part, and if none of the cake adheres to it, it is baked enough. When cake that is baked on flat tins, moves easily on them it is sufficiently done.

140. Gingerbread.

Melt a piece of butter, of the size of a hen's egg and put it with a pint of molasses, stir in a little flour, and a heaping table spoonful of ginger. Dissolve a large table spoonful of saleratus, in half a pint of water, strain and mix it with the rest of the ingredients, together with flour enough to enable you to roll it out easily. Roll it about half an inch thick, and lay it on flat buttered tins; bake it as soon as rolled out in a quick oven a few moments. Gingerbread to be very nice, should be made of good molasses, and baked very quick. Some people use only a tea spoonful of saleratus, to a pint of molasses, but it is much better with more, appearing in point of lightness like sponge cake.

141. Soft Gingerbread.

Melt a cup of butter and mix it with a pint of molasses, a table spoonful of ginger and a little flour, dissolve three tea spoonsful of saleratus, in a tea cup of water, and stir it into the cake, together with flour enough to render it of the consistency of pound cake. Bake it in deep cake pans, about thirty minutes. A couple of eggs improve the cake.

142. Ginger Snaps.

Mix half a tea cup of melted butter, with a tea cup of sugar, half a tea cup of molasses, and a table spoonful of ginger. Dissolve a tea spoonful of saleratus, in half a tea cup of water and strain it into the cake, knead in flour till quite stiff. Roll it out very thin, and cut it into cakes, with a wine glass. Lay them on buttered tins, and bake them a few moments, in a very moderate oven. A tea spoonful of allspice, the same quantity of cinnamon, mace, and coriander seed, together with a tea spoonful of ginger instead of a table spoonful, put into this cake will convert it into spice snaps.

143. Cider Cake.

Rub together three quarters of a pound of sugar, and half a pound of butter. Dissolve two tea spoonsful of saleratus in half a tea cup of water, turn it into the cake, together with half a pint of cider, stir in two pounds of flour and a grated nutmeg. Bake it about half an hour. This cake should be eaten in the course of two or three days after it is made, as it gets dry very quick.

144. Cookies.

Stir together one cup of butter, two of sugar. Dissolve a tea spoonful of saleratus in a cup of milk, (water will do but the cake will not be as rich,) stir it into the cake, together with a table spoonful of caraway seed, and one egg beaten to a froth, knead in flour till of the right consistency to roll out easily. Lay the cake on a moulding board, and if you cannot roll it out without its sticking to the rolling pin, more flour should be added. Stamp and cut it into cakes, lay them on flat tins well buttered, bake them in a quick oven.

145. New Year's Cookies.

Mix one pound of butter, a pound and three quarters of sugar, dissolve a couple of tea spoonsful of saleratus, in a pint of milk, and turn it on to the butter and sugar when well mixed, beat three eggs to a froth and stir them into the cake, with a grated nutmeg, and three heaping table spoonsful of caraway seed. Sift three pounds of flour and work into the cake with the hand. Roll them half an inch thick, and bake them immediately in a quick oven.

146. Plain Tea Cakes.

Stir together half a tea cup of butter, two of sugar, turn in a tea cup of milk with a tea spoonful of saleratus dissolved in it, add one half of a grated nutmeg, and flour enough to enable you to roll it out, cut it into small cakes.

147. Shrewsbury Cake.

Mix a pound of butter, with twelve ounces of sugar, add five eggs beaten to a froth, a little rosewater, or essence of lemon, and a pound of flour, roll the cake out thin, and stamp and cut it into cakes, and bake them in a quick oven.

148. Tunbridge Cake.

Stir six ounces of butter with the same quantity of sugar, beat a couple of eggs and put in, together with a table spoonful of cream, and a little orange flower water, or essence of lemon; add three quarters of a pound of flour, roll it out thin and cut it into cakes.

149. Jumbles.

Mix half a pound of sugar, with the same quantity of butter, five beaten eggs, a little essence of lemon; add a pound of flour when well mixed. Roll it about half an inch thick, cut it into narrow strips of equal length, join the ends together so as to form rings. Bake them on flat tins.

150. Simbals.

Rub together half a pound of sugar, quarter of a pound of butter; dissolve a tea spoonful of saleratus, in half a cup of milk, put it into the cake, with a couple of beaten eggs, a little mace or nutmeg. Then add flour enough to render it sufficiently stiff, to roll out. It should be rolled in pounded white sugar, cut into strips, and the ends joined in the form of rings.

151. Sugar Gingerbread.

Mix a pound of sugar with six ounces of butter, dissolve a tea spoonful of saleratus, in half a tumbler of milk, and stir in, together with four beaten eggs, three tea spoonsful of ginger;

when well mixed, add a pound and a half of flour, and roll it out about an inch thick, run a jagging iron across it, in parallel lines, an inch apart. Bake it on flat buttered tins, in a quick oven.

152. Rusk.

Melt six ounces of butter, and mix it with half a pound of sugar, turn in half a pint of lukewarm milk, half a tea cup of yeast, (brewer's is the best,) add three tea spoonsful of cinnamon, and flour to make them stiff enough to mould up. Set them in a warm place to rise. When light mould them up into small cakes, lay them on tins well buttered, let them remain till very light, before baking them.

153. Whigs.

Mix three quarters of a pound of sugar, with half a pound of butter; when white, beat two eggs, and put in, together with half a pint of milk, half a tea cup of yeast, a tea spoonful of rosewater or nutmeg, and two pounds of flour. When very light bake them in cups.

154. Hot Cream Cakes.

Rub together three quarters of a pound of flour, a quarter of a pound of butter, and half a tea spoonful of salt; beat four eggs to a froth, and put in, together with a tea cup of cream; drop this mixture into buttered muffin hoops, placed in a buttered bake pan; when brown take them up, split and butter them.

155. Cross Buns.

Mix a tumbler of lukewarm milk, with a pint of flour, a tea cup of yeast, a tea spoonful of salt, the same quantity of allspice, mace, and three tea spoonsful of cinnamon, set it in a warm place; when light, add half a pound of sugar, the same quantity of melted butter, (it should not be hot,) and flour enough to render it sufficiently stiff to roll out. Put them in a warm place to rise again, when risen mould them up into cakes, of the size of an egg, lay them on buttered tins several inches apart; press on them a mould in the form of a cross, let them remain an hour before baking them.

156. Nut Cakes.

Melt a tea cup of lard, and mix it with four tea cups of rolled sugar, three eggs well beaten, three tea spoonsful of cinnamon, or a little rosewater, add a pint of lukewarm milk, half a pint of yeast, and flour to make it stiff enough to roll out. Put it in a warm place to rise, (the oven is the best place to raise them in, several hours after you have baked in it.) When so light as to appear like a sponge in the middle, roll it out about an inch thick, and cut it into cakes about three inches long and two wide; let them stand twenty or thirty minutes before boiling them. Fry them in a kettle, with about two pounds of hot lard; the fat should boil up as they are put in, and not more than seven or eight boiled at once; the kettle should be over a brisk fire and shaken constantly while frying. The same lard will answer to fry several

batches of nut cakes in, if not burnt, with
the addition of a little more fat.

157. Crollers.

Melt your lard in a frying pan, to fry
your crollers in; take four table spoonsful
of it when melted, and mix with five
heaping table spoonsful of rolled sugar,
half a tea spoonful of salt, four beaten
eggs, and a little essence of lemon, or
rosewater. Dissolve a tea spoonful of
saleratus, in half a tea cup of milk, and
turn it in, together with flour sufficient to
enable you to roll it out easily. Roll it half
an inch thick, cut it with a jagging iron, or
knife, into strips about half an inch wide,
twist them into any shape you please.
Heat your fat in your frying pan till it boils
up, as the cakes are laid in. There
should be fat enough, to cover them,
watch them narrowly, when brown on
the under side, turn them carefully and
let them brown on the other.

158. Molasses Dough Cake.

Into three tea cups of raised dough,
work with the hand half a tea cup of
melted butter, a tea cup of molasses,
and a couple of eggs, beaten to a froth,
chop the rind of a fresh lemon very fine,
and put it in, together with the juice, and
a tea spoonful of cinnamon; work it with
the hand eight or ten minutes, then put it
into cake pans well buttered, and set it in
a warm place, about twenty minutes
before baking it.

159. Sugar Dough Cake.

Dissolve a tea spoonful of saleratus

in half a tumbler of milk, strain it on three cups of raised dough, a tea cup of melted butter, two eggs, two tea cups of rolled sugar, and two tea spoonsful of cinnamon. Work it with the hand, for ten or twelve minutes, put it in deep pans, set it in a warm place for fifteen minutes before you put it in the oven.

160. Measure Cake.

Stir together till of a light color, a tea cup of butter, with two of sugar, beat four eggs and put in, together with a grated nutmeg, and a pint of flour. Stir it till just before it goes into the oven, bake it in deep tins about twenty minutes.

161. Cup Cake.

Mix three cups of sugar, with one and a half of butter. Beat three eggs and put in, together with a little essence of lemon, or rosewater. Dissolve a tea spoonful of saleratus, in a tea cup of milk, and strain it into the cake. Stir in six cups of sifted flour, and bake it either in cups or deep pans.

162. French Loaf.

Stir together one pound of sugar, three quarters of butter. When white, mix a gill of wine, one of rose or French brandy, half a gill of milk and stir it into the cake, together with eight eggs beaten to a froth, the whites and yolks separate, put in a pound and a half of sifted flour, just before it goes into the oven; add a grated nutmeg, a quarter of a pound of citron, or pounded almonds, and three quarters of a pound of Zante currants or stoned raisins.

163. Washington Cake.

Dissolve a tea spoonful of saleratus in a wine glass of milk, and put it with half a pound of butter and a pound of sugar previously stirred white, add a wine glass of wine, four eggs, and a pound and a half of flour, put in rosewater or essence of lemon, to the taste.

164. Plain Cream Cake.

Mix a tea cup of cream, two of sugar, a couple of beaten eggs, and a wine glass of milk, with a tea spoonful of saleratus dissolved in it. Stir in flour to render it of the consistency of pound cake.

165. Rich Cream Cake.

Stir till white, half a pound of butter, with three quarters of sugar, then add a wine glass of brandy, seven eggs beaten to a froth, the whites and yolks separate. Stir in a pound and a half of sifted flour, and mace to your taste. Just before it goes into the oven stir in half a pint of cream, and three quarters of a pound of fruit.

166. Shelah or quick Loaf Cake.

Melt half a pound of butter, when cool work it into a pound and a half of raised dough. Beat four eggs, with three quarters of a pound of rolled sugar, and put it into the cake together with a tea spoonful of saleratus, dissolved in a tea cup of milk, add a wine glass of brandy, a little mace and cinnamon. Work the whole with the hand for a quarter of an hour, add a pound of raisins; then put it into cake pans, let it remain twenty five or thirty minutes, before baking it.

167. Loaf Cake.

Into two pounds of flour, stir a pound of lukewarm melted butter and a tea cup of yeast, put it in a warm place to rise, but care must be taken not to get it too warm, as the yeast will get scalded, and prevent its rising. When perfectly light, beat four eggs with a pound and a quarter of sugar, and work them into the sponge, with a wine glass of wine, and one of brandy, three tea spoonsful of cinnamon, a little mace, or nutmeg. Work the whole well with the hand for ten minutes, then set it where it will rise again. When risen the second time, work it with the hand for fifteen minutes, then stir in gradually a pound of stoned raisins, and quarter of a pound of citron cut into small strips, fill your cake pans about half full, put them near the fire for half an hour, to rise again in the pans. Bake the cake in a quick (but not a furious oven,) for about an hour and twenty minutes.

168. Rice Cake.

Mix ten ounces of ground rice, three of wheat flour, eight ounces of powdered sugar, sift them by degrees into eight yolks and six whites of eggs previously beaten to a froth, grate in the peel of a lemon, and bake it in deep pans, about twenty minutes.

169. Diet Bread.

Sift a pound of flour, and put it with a pound of sugar and eight eggs well beaten, add a little rosewater or essence of lemon, bake it fifteen or twenty minutes.

170. Scotch or Lemon Cake.

Stir together till white, a pound of sugar, half a pound of butter; then put in eight eggs, beaten to a froth, with the grated peel of a couple of lemons, and the juice. Sift a pound of flour and stir it in.

171. Pound Cake.

Mix a pound of sugar, three quarters of butter, when white put in eight eggs beaten to a froth, the whites and yolks separate, add a pound of sifted flour, and mace, to your taste. If you wish your cake to be very rich, stir in just before it is put in the oven, half a pound of stoned raisins, and quarter of a pound of citron, or pounded sweet almonds.

172. Queen's or Heart Cakes.

Rub together till very white, a pound of sugar, three quarters of butter, then beat the whites and yolks of seven eggs, separately to a froth, and stir them into the cake, mix a wine glass of wine, one of brandy, and one of milk, turn it into the cake, then stir in a pound of flour, a little essence of lemon, and mace or nutmeg to your taste. Stir the whole well together, then add (a minute before you put it in the pans,) half a pound of raisins seeded, quarter of a pound of Zante currants, quarter of a pound of almonds pounded fine, or citron cut in strips; they should be stirred in very gradually, a handful of each alternately; when well mixed in, bake the cake immediately, in small tins or in large cake pans, if baked in the latter it will require baking about an hour and twenty five minutes, if baked in small tins it will bake in much less time.

173. Jelly Cake.

Stir together half a pound of sugar, and six ounces of butter, beat seven eggs to a froth and put in, together with a little mace, or nutmeg, then stir in gradually a pound of flour, and the juice and grated peel of a fresh lemon, turn the mixture on to scolloped tin plates, well buttered, the mixture should not be more than quarter of an inch thick in each one, bake them until brown, in a quick oven, then pile them together on a plate, with jelly spread on each one and jelly on the top.

174. Raised Queen's Cake.

Stir into a pound of flour, half a pint of lukewarm milk, a tea cup of yeast, set it in a warm place; when light stir a pound of sugar, with three quarters of butter and work it into the sponge, with three beaten eggs, a little mace or essence of lemon, and half a pound more of sifted flour. Work the whole together for fifteen or twenty minutes, then let it remain till very light, when so, stir in half a pound of seeded raisins, quarter of a pound of Zante currants, and the same of citron. Bake it directly in a moderate oven, but not a slow one.

175. Sponge Cake.

Take the weight of ten eggs, in sifted loaf sugar, beat it well with the yolks of twelve eggs, then grate in the peel of a fresh lemon, and add the juice of half an one. Beat the whites of six eggs to a froth, and mix them with the sugar and yolks. Beat the whole, well together without any cessation, for fifteen minutes, on a shallow plate, then stir in very gradually the weight of six eggs, in sifted flour, put it in a moderate oven, as soon as the flour is well mixed in, and bake it from fifteen to twenty minutes.

176. Almond Sponge Cake.

Into the whites of sixteen eggs, beaten to a froth, stir their weight of sifted loaf sugar; beat them well five or six minutes, then add the weight of seven whites of eggs, in sweet almonds, previously blanched, dried, and pounded fine, a table spoonful of cream or lukewarm melted butter, beat the ingredients well together, then stir in very gradually, the weight of the whites of eight eggs, in sifted flour; as soon as it is mixed in well, bake it in a moderate oven about twenty minutes.

177. Black or Fruit Cake.

Stir for twenty minutes, four pounds of butter with five of sugar. Beat forty eggs, the whites and yolks separate, and stir them into the butter and sugar, then add a table spoonful of cinnamon, the same quantity of rosewater, a tea spoonful of essence of lemon, or three of orange flower water, half an ounce of allspice, the same of mace, and a tea spoonful of cloves. Stir in very gradually, five pound of sifted flour. Mix three glasses of white wine, three of brandy, and two of milk. Stir it with the rest of the above ingredients for twenty minutes, then stir in three quarters of a pound of blanched, dried and pounded almonds, four pounds of stoned raisins, five of Zante currants, and a pound of citron, cut in small pieces, the fruit should be stirred in gradually, a handful of each kind alternately. Bake it immediately in a moderate oven, for about two hours and a half. This kind of cake will keep good four or five months.

178. Almond Cheese Cake.

Mix half a pound of powdered loaf sugar, with four ounces of butter, when white add a gill of cream, if you have it, if not put in the same quantity of boiling milk, with an ounce of pounded cracker, two ounces of blanched and pounded sweet almonds, half a glass of wine, a tea spoonful of orange flower or rosewater, and half a grated nutmeg. Beat five eggs to a froth, the whites and yolks separate, and stir into the above mixture; then set it on a few coals and stir it constantly till scalding hot, take it off before it boils, and stir it till nearly cold, then add quarter of a pound of Zante currants. Pour it into patty pans, lined with puff paste, cut blanched almonds into small slips, and ornament the top of the cheese cake with them. Bake them in a quick oven twenty minutes.

179. Maccaroons.

Beat the whites of nine eggs to a stiff froth, then stir in ten large table spoonsful of powdered loaf sugar, beat them together well; add quarter of a pound of bitter almonds, previously blanched, dried and pounded fine, and the same quantity of sweet ones. When the whole is well mixed, do them up into balls of the size of a walnut, lay them on buttered baking plates, several inches apart, flatten them on the top, bake them in a slow oven till of a light brown.

180. Frosting for Cake.

Allow for each loaf of cake, the white of one egg, and ten heaping tea spoonsful of powdered double refined loaf sugar. Beat the eggs on a shallow plate till you can turn the plate upside down, without the eggs dropping from it. Then stir in the sugar very gradually; stir it without any cessation for fifteen minutes, then add a tea spoonful of lemon juice, vinegar will do but it is not as good as the lemon juice. If you wish to have it colored, stir in a few grains of cochineal powder, or a little powder blue. As soon as you have put in the lemon juice, lay it with a knife, on the cake, which should be hot, smooth it over, and set the cake away in a cool place, and let it remain, until it hardens.

181. Cocoanut Cakes.

Beat the whites of eight eggs, to a stiff froth, then stir in half a pound of sifted loaf sugar; it should be stirred in very gradually, and beaten eight or ten minutes, then add half a pound of grated cocoanut, the brown part should be cut off before it is grated. Put in a table spoonful of the milk of the cocoanut, if you have it, if not it will do without, drop it on buttered pie plates, several inches apart, the drops should be about the size of a cent. Bake them in a oven about twenty minutes.

182. Floating Island.

Beat the whites of nine eggs to a froth, then beat with them seven large table spoonsful of whatever dark colored jelly, you may happen to have. When you have beaten them seven or eight minutes, put some cream into a large shallow dish, and turn the jelly and eggs, into the center of it. This should not be made but a short time before it is to be eaten.

183. Whip Syllabub.

Take good sweet cream, and to each pint of it, put six ounces of sifted double refined loaf sugar, half a tumbler of white wine, the juice and grated peel of a lemon. Beat it well, as the froth rises, take it off and lay it on jelly, in a dish or glasses. Keep it in a cool place till just before it is eaten.

184. Blanc Mange.

Pull an ounce of isinglass, into small

pieces, rinse and put it to a pint and a half of milk. Stir it over a slow fire, with a stick of cinnamon or mace, and loaf sugar to your taste. Stir it without boiling until the isinglass dissolves. Then set it where it will boil five or six minutes, stirring it constantly. Strain it and fill your moulds with it when cool, and let it remain until wanted.

185. Rice Flour Blanc Mange.

Boil a quart of milk and sweeten it to your taste with loaf sugar; add the juice and grated peel of a lemon. Mix four table spoonsful of ground rice smoothly with a little cold milk, and stir it into the boiling milk. Boil the whole together ten minutes, stirring it occasionally while boiling; then take it from the fire, stir into it the beaten whites of three eggs, set it back on a few coals, and stir it constantly until nearly boiling hot, take it off, fill your moulds, and let it remain till cold. This is very good food for invalids.

186. Ice Cream.

To one quart of milk, put the yolks of four eggs well beaten, the rind of a lemon pared thin, sweeten it very sweet with loaf sugar. Put it on a slow fire and stir it constantly till scalding hot, care must be taken then it does not get to boiling. Take it up, take out the lemon peel, set it away to cool. When perfectly cold put it into an ice cream form, (if you cannot procure one, a milk kettle will do,) set it into a large tub, strew round it a layer of ice cracked fine, then a layer of rock salt, then another layer of ice and salt, and so on, till the ice is as high as the top of the form; a layer of ice should be last. Shake the form frequently, while the cream is freezing; care must be taken that none of the salt gets into the cream. The tub should be covered with a flannel cloth, while the cream is freezing. If you wish to shape the cream in moulds, turn it into them, as soon as it freezes in the form, and set them in the tub, and let them remain in it, till just before they are to be eaten. When you wish to get them out of the moulds or form, dip them into warm water and take them out of it instantly and turn them out into your dishes. Where cream is used instead of milk, no eggs or scalding will be necessary. Three table spoonsful of pine apple juice, to a quart of the cream gives it a fine flavor, strawberries are also nice in the cream. If you wish to color the cream, stir in a little cochineal powder, saffron or powder blue, before you freeze it.

187. Pastry.

For good common pie crust, allow two tea cups of shortening to a quart of flour, and a tea spoonful of salt, half lard and half butter is the best, beef shortening does very well with butter for plain pie crust. Rub part of the shortening thoroughly with two thirds of the flour; then put in the salt, together with cold water, to moisten it just enough to roll out easily. Roll it out thin, spread on the reserved shortening, then sprinkle on the remainder of your flour, and roll it up. Cut it into as many pieces as you have pies, roll out the under crust very thin, butter your pie plates, and put it on them, fill your plates with your fruit, roll out the upper crust lightly, about half an inch thick, and cover your pies, pare it off neatly round the edges of the plates. This rule furnishes crust enough for a couple of pies. Pie crust to be light, should be baked in a quick oven.

188. Puff Paste or Confectioner's Pastry.

Sift three quarters of a pound of flour, and mix it with cold water enough to render it sufficiently stiff to roll out, put in one half a tea spoonful of salt, before you put in the water. Weigh out a pound of butter, cut it into thin slices, and roll it out thin as possible on a moulding board; in order to do this a great deal of flour should be sprinkled on the board and butter, and rubbed on the rolling pin. Lay your rolled butter on a platter. Then roll out your crust very thin, lay the pieces of butter thickly over it. Weigh out a quarter of a pound of sifted flour, and sprinkle part of it over it, roll it up, then roll it out again, put on the remainder of the butter and flour, roll it up and let it stand half an hour in a cool place. Roll it our lightly half an inch thick, for the upper crust to the pies. Bake it in a quick oven till of a light brown.

189. Apple Pie.

Pare, quarter, and take out the cores of the apples, and if not ripe, stew them before baking them, and season them to your taste. Butter your plates, put on a thin under crust, fill the plates, and cover them with a thick crust. Bake them about three quarters of an hour. When done take off the upper crust carefully, and put a piece of butter of the size of a walnut, into each pie, sweeten them to your taste, if not acid enough, squeeze in the juice of part of a lemon, or put in a little tartaric acid, dissolved in a little water. Essence of lemon, nutmeg, or rosewater, are all good spice for apple pies. Apples stewed in new cider, and molasses, with a few quinces and strained, with a little cinnamon in it makes nice pies. Dried apples for pies, should have boiling water turned on them, and stewed till tender, then add a little sour cider, and a little orange peel, and stew them a few moments longer, take them up, put in a little butter, sugar, and the juice and peel of a lemon improve them, they are better for being rubbed through a sieve. Fill your pie plates and bake the pies half an hour.

190. Mince Pie.

The best kind of meat for mince pies, is neats tongue and feet, and chickens; a shank of beef makes very good pies. Boil your meat till perfectly tender, then take it up, clear it from the bones and gristle, chop it very fine and mix it with double the quantity of chopped apple; if the meat is not fat, put in a little suet or melted butter, moisten it with cider, add cloves, mace, or nutmeg, and cinnamon, to your taste, sweeten it with molasses and sugar, add a little salt. If you wish to have your pies very rich, put in wine or brandy to your taste, the juice and peel of a lemon, the peel should be grated, and stoned raisins and citron cut in small strips. Bake the pies in shallow plates. Make apertures in the upper crust, before you cover the pies. Bake the pies from half, to three quarters of an hour. Mince meat for pies, with brandy or wine in it, and strongly spiced will keep several months, in cold weather. It should be put in a stone pot, and kept in a dry cool place.

191. Peach Pie.

Take mellow juicy peaches, wash and put them in a deep pie plate, or pudding dish, lined with pie crust, sprinkle sugar on each layer of peaches, a great deal will be necessary to sweeten them sufficiently, put in about a table spoonful of water, sprinkle a little flour over the top and cover the pie with a thick crust. Bake it an hour. Pies made in this manner are much better than with the stones taken out, as the prussic acid of the stones, gives the pie a fine flavor. Dried peaches should be stewed and sweetened, before being made into pies; they do not require any spice.

192. Tart Pie.

Sour apples, cranberries, and dried peaches, all make nice tarts. Stew and strain them; if the peaches are not tart, put in the juice and grated peel of a lemon, put in a little sugar. Line shallow pie plates with a thin crust, put a rim of pie crust round the edge of the dish, fill the plates with your tart. Roll some of the crust very thin, cut it into narrow strips, with a jagging iron, and lay it on the pie in a fanciful manner. Bake the pies about twenty five minutes.

193. Rice Pie.

To a quart of boiling water, put a small tea cup of rice, and boil it till very soft. Then add a quart of milk, strain it through a sieve, put in a little salt, five beaten eggs, a nutmeg grated, and sugar enough to sweeten it, the sugar should be put in before the rice is strained, add a few raisins. Bake it in deep pie plates, without an upper crust.

194. Rhubarb or Persian Apple Pie.

Take the stalks of the rhubarb plant in the spring, or fore part of summer, (they are not good later,) cut them in small pieces, and stew them till tender; then strain and sweeten them to your taste, bake them with only an under crust.

195. Cherry and Blackberry Pies.

Cherries and blackberries for pies, should be perfectly ripe; put them in a deep plate, with an under crust, and sprinkle sugar and cinnamon, or cloves, over them; cover them and bake them half an hour.

196. Grape Pie.

Grapes are the best for pies when very small and tender; if not very small, they should be stewed and strained, on account of the seeds. Sweeten them to your taste, no spice is necessary.

197. Currant and Gooseberry Pies.

Pick them over, and stew them in just water enough to prevent their burning at the bottom, when tender sweeten them to your taste with sugar, and bake them without any spice, in deep dishes. Some people do not stew the currants before baking them, but they are not apt to be sweet enough, if not previously stewed.

198. Pumpkin Pie.

Cut your pumpkin in two, take out the seeds, and wash the pumpkin, cut it into small strips, and boil it in just water enough to prevent its burning, when tender turn off the water, and let it steam over a moderate fire for fifteen minutes, taking care it does not burn. Take it up, strain it through the sieve, and if you like the pies very thin, put two quarts of milk, to a quart of the pumpkin, and six eggs; if you wish to have them thick, put a quart only of milk, to a quart of pumpkin, and three eggs. Three eggs to a quart of milk does very well, but they are better with five or six. Sweeten it with molasses or sugar, put in ginger, or grated lemon peel to your taste. Bake them in deep plates from fifty to sixty minutes in a hot oven.

199. Carrot Pie.

Scrape three good sized carrots, boil them till very tender. Then rub them through a sieve, and mix them with a quart of milk, four beaten eggs, a piece of butter of the size of half an egg, a table spoonful of lemon juice, and the

grated peel of half a one. Sweeten it to
your taste. Bake it in deep pie plates
with an under crust and rim.

200. Potatoe Pie.

Boil Irish or sweet potatoes, till very
soft. Take them up, peel and mash them
fine. To one quarter of a pound of
potatoes put a quart of milk, three
ounces of butter, melted; five eggs, a
glass of wine, and one of lemon or
French brandy. Put in sugar, and mace
to your taste.

201. Marlborough Pie.

Pare tart mellow apples, quarter
them, take out the seeds, and stew them
in a little water till soft enough to rub
through a sieve. To twelve table
spoonsful of it when strained, put twelve
table spoonsful of sugar, the same
quantity of wine, five eggs, six table
spoonsful of melted butter, half a pint of
milk, the juice and grated peel of half a
lemon, and half a nutmeg. Bake it in
deep pie plates, without an upper crust.

202. Custard Pie.

Beat seven eggs with three table
spoonsful of rolled sugar, mix them with
a quart of milk, flavor it with nutmeg or
rosewater. This is good baked either in
cups, or deep pie plates, with an under
crust. Set the pie plates with the crust in
the oven and let it bake a moment
before you turn in the custard. To
ascertain when the pie is done, stick a
clean broom splinter through the center
of the pie, if none of the custard adheres

to it, it is sufficiently bakes.

203. A Plain Custard Pie.

Boil a quart of milk with a few peach leaves, or lemon peel; strain it. Put it back on the fire; when it boils, mix a table spoonful of flour, with a little milk, and turn it in, let it boil a minute, then put it with four beaten eggs, and sugar to your taste, and bake it in deep pie plates with an under crust.

204. Lemon Pie.

Squeeze out the juice of two good sized lemons, grate the rind of the lemon, but not the white part, put the juice and grated lemon to a pint of milk. Beat six eggs, with five table spoonsful of powdered loaf sugar, and put them in the milk, with a couple of crackers pounded fine, and a table spoonful of melted butter. Line a pudding dish with pie crust, put a rim of puff paste, or nice pie crust, round the edge, turn the mixture into it, and bake it from twenty five to thirty minutes.

205. Cocoanut Pie.

Cut off the brown part of the cocoanut, grate the remainder of it. Scald a quart of milk, and turn it on to the cocoanut, and three crackers pounded fine. Beat eight eggs, with three table spoonsful of sifted loaf sugar, turn it into the milk, together with a glass of wine, and half a grated nutmeg. If any of the milk of the cocoanut can be saved, to mix with the cow's milk, it makes the pie nicer. Bake it in a deep pie plate, or pudding dish, with a rim of puff paste round the edge of the dish.

206. Small Puffs.

Make some puff paste, and roll it half an inch thick, cut it with a tumbler, into any number of puffs you want, cut the remainder of your paste, into narrow strips with a jagging iron, put them round the edge of those you have cut with a tumbler, lay the puffs on buttered plates, and bake them in a quick oven, till of a light brown. Then fill them with any preserved fruit, you may happen to have.

207. Boiled Custards.

Boil a quart of milk. Beat six eggs with three table spoonsful of sugar, four eggs are enough if you want them plain, grate in a nutmeg, or put in a little rosewater, or essence of lemon. Turn the boiling milk on to the sugar and eggs, stir it several minutes then put it on a few coals, stir it constantly till boiling hot, take it up before it gets to boiling, stir it a few moments, then turn it into your cups and grate nutmeg on them.

208. Almond Custards.

Boil in a quart of milk, a couple of ounces each of sweet, and of bitter almonds, pounded fine. When it has boiled seven or eight minutes strain it on to the beaten yolks of eight eggs, and three table spoonsful of loaf sugar. Stir it several moments, then put it on a moderate fire, stir it without any cessation till scalding hot, then take it from the fire, and stir it constantly till nearly cold, then fill your glasses or cups. Just before they are to be eaten, beat the whites of the eggs, to a froth, and lay them on the top of the custards. A few grains of cochineal powder, or saffron in the beaten whites, makes them look handsomely.

209. Cold Custard or Rennet Pudding.

Put a piece of calf's rennet three inches square, to a pint of wine, when it has stood seven or eight hours, it is fit for use. Whenever you wish to make your custard, put three table spoonsful of the wine, to a quart of milk, and four table spoonsful of powdered loaf sugar, flavor it with essence of lemon, or rosewater. Stir it twenty minutes, then dish it out, grate nutmeg over it. It should be eaten in the course of an hour after it is made, as it will soon curdle.

210. Custard Pudding.

Stir a quart of milk very gradually into half a pint of flour, put in a little salt, seven beaten eggs, and a little nutmeg or essence of lemon, sweeten it to your taste, bake it three quarters of an hour.

211. Boiled Bread Pudding.

Soak about three quarters of a pound of rusked bread, in milk, if you have not milk, water will do. When soft, squeeze out the water, mash it fine and put in a heaping table spoonful of flour, mixed with a tea cup of milk, put in three eggs, half a tea spoonful of salt. Mix the whole well together, flour the inside of your pudding bag, and put the pudding in. The bag should not be more than two thirds full, as the pudding swells considerably while boiling. The pudding should be put into a pot of boiling water, and boiled an hour and a half without intermission; if allowed to stop it will be heavy.

212. A Plain Baked Bread Pudding.

Pound rusked bread, and put five heaping table spoonsful of it to a quart of milk, three beaten eggs, four table spoonsful of sugar, half a tea spoonful of salt, half a nutmeg, and a table spoonful of melted butter. Bake it an hour and a half; it is good without the eggs, if baked two hours and a half. It does not require any sauce.

213. A Rich Bread Pudding.

Cut a loaf of baker's bread into thin slices, spread butter on both sides; lay them in a buttered pudding dish, and on each layer strew Zante currants, or stoned raisins, and citron cut into small pieces. Beat eight eggs with six table spoonsful of sugar rolled free from lumps; mix them with three pints of milk, and a grated nutmeg. Turn the whole over the bread and let it stand until the bread has absorbed most of the milk, then bake it about three quarters of an hour.

214. Flour Pudding.

Into a pint and a half of flour, stir gradually a quart of milk; stir it till free from lumps, then add seven beaten eggs, a couple of tea spoonsful of salt, and a grated nutmeg. A pudding made in this manner is good either baked or boiled; it takes two hours to boil and one to bake it. It should be eaten as soon as cooked or it will be heavy. This as well as all other kinds of boiled puddings should not be put into the pot until the water boils and should not be allowed to stop for a moment, if the water wastes much in boiling, fill the pot up with boiling water. A pudding bag should be floured on the inside, and not filled more than two thirds full. When the pudding has boiled six or eight minutes turn it over, as it is apt to settle. Flour puddings require rich sauce.

215. A Plain Rice Pudding.

Swell the rice with a little milk over a fire, then put in acid apples pared and cut in thin slices, or gooseberries and currants, add a couple of eggs, a tea spoonful of salt, fill your pudding bag half full and boil it an hour and a half. Serve it up with butter and sugar.

216. A Rich Rice Pudding.

Pick over and wash two small tea cups of rice and put it into two quarts of milk; add a tea cup of butter, two of sugar, and a grated nutmeg. Butter a pudding dish, set it in a bake pan, then turn in the pudding, when it begins to thicken stir in three tea cups full of raisins. Bake it two hours, it will not fall if taken from the fire sometime before it is to be eaten, it is also good cold. It is good without any sauce, and is the only kind of pudding that eggs do not improve.

217. Rice Snow Balls.

Pare large tart apples, take out the cores with a pen-knife; fill the holes with sugar, and a stick of cinnamon or mace. Put each one in a small bag well floured, fill them half full of unboiled rice, tie up the bags and boil them an hour and twenty minutes. When done turn them out carefully and serve them up with pudding sauce.

218. Baked Indian Pudding.

Boil three pints of milk, and turn it on to a pint of Indian meal, and five table spoonsful of wheat flour. When cool beat three eggs with the same quantity of sugar, and stir it into the pudding, together with a tea spoonful of salt, three tea spoonsful of cinnamon, and a piece of butter of the size of an egg. If raisins are put in the pudding, a tea cup more of milk will be required, as they absorb the milk. This pudding is good if the eggs are omitted. It takes two hours and a half to bake it.

219. Boiled Indian Pudding.

Into a quart of boiling milk, stir a couple of table spoonsful of flour, and sifted Indian meal till it is a thick batter, and half a table spoonful of ginger or cinnamon, half a tea cup of molasses. Dip the pudding bag into water, wring it out, and flour the inside of it, and fill it not more than half full, as Indian puddings swell very much. Put it into boiling water, and keep it boiling constantly for four or five hours. A kettle of boiling water should be kept, to turn into the pudding pot as the water boils away.

220. Corn Pudding.

Grate a cup and a half of green corn, mix it with a quart of milk, four beaten eggs, and half a grated nutmeg; melt a piece of butter of the size of a hen's egg, and stir it in. Bake it one hour.

221. Hasty Pudding.

Wet Indian meal with cold water sufficient to make a thin batter, turn part of it into a pot of boiling water; when it has boiled fifteen or twenty minutes stir in the remainder, salt it to your taste, and stir in Indian meal by the handful as long as you can stir the pudding stick round in it easily. When the stick can be made to stand upright in it for a minute, it is thick enough. It should boil slowly, and be stirred often; if you wish to fry it, it will be necessary to boil it, from two to three hours, if not it will boil sufficiently in an hour. If a little flour is stirred in just before it is taken up, it will fry better. Turn it into a deep dish, and if it is to be fried, let it stand till cold, then cut it into thin slices, flour and fry them in lard, till very brown.

222. Fruit Pudding.

Take raised or common pie crust, and roll it out about half an inch thick. Strew over it either currants, cherries, cranberries, gooseberries, black or whortle berries. Sprinkle sugar, and cinnamon or cloves over them. Roll it up carefully, join the ends together, and put it in a floured cloth and sew it up. Boil it an hour, and eat it with sauce as soon as done.

223. Fritters.

Mix a quart of milk gradually, with a quart of flour, stir it till smooth, then add a little essence of lemon, or rosewater, and five beaten eggs. Drop it into boiling hot fat by the spoonsful. They are lighter for being fried in a great deal of fat, but less greasy if fried in just enough to prevent their sticking to the griddle. They should be served up with pudding sauce.

224. Apple Dumplings.

Make good common, or raised pie crust, divide it into as many pieces, as you wish dumplings. Pare tart mellow apples, take out the cores, with a penknife, fill the holes with a blade of mace, and sugar. Roll out your crust half an inch thick, and enclose an apple in each piece. Tie them up in separate bags, that are floured inside. Drop them into a pot of boiling water, and boil them without any intermission for an hour, then take them out of the bags. If allowed to stop boiling they will not be light. Eat them with butter and sugar, or pudding sauce.

225. Orange Pudding.

Mix three ounces of butter, with four

table spoonsful of powdered loaf sugar, when stirred to a cream, add a quart of boiling milk, the juice and peel of two large oranges, the peel should be chopped very fine, put in a gill of wine, then an ounce of citron, cut into small strips, add eight eggs, the whiles and yolks beaten separately. Mix the whole well together, then turn it into a pudding dish, with a lining and rim of puff paste. Bake it directly in a quick oven from twenty-five to thirty minutes.

226. Bird's Nest Pudding.

Pare and halve tart mellow apples, scoop out the cores, put a little flour in the hollow of the apples, and wet it so as to form a thick paste, stick a blade or two of mace and three or four Zante currants, in each one of the apples. Butter small cups, and put half an apple, in each one, lay three or four narrow strips of citron round each apple. Mix a quart of milk, with three table spoonsful of flour, six eggs, a grated nutmeg and four table spoonsful of sugar. Nearly fill the cups with this mixture. Bake them about thirty minutes. They should be eaten as soon as done.

227. Apple Custard Pudding.

Pare and take out the cores of nice tart apples, lay them in a pudding dish, well buttered, fill the holes of the apples, with nutmeg and sugar. For nine or ten apples, mix half a pint of flour with a quart of milk, four table spoonsful of sugar, and seven eggs, turn it over the apples, flavor it with whatever spice you like, and bake it about half an hour.

228. English Plum Pudding.

Soak three quarters of a pound of finely pounded crackers in two quarts of milk. Put in twelve beaten eggs, half a pound of stoned raisins, quarter of a pound of Zante currants, the same weight of citron, cut into small pieces, and five ounces of blanched and pounded almonds; add a wine glass of lemon brandy, or wine, and a little orange flower, or rosewater, and a little salt. Bake or boil it from two hours and a half, to three hours.

229. Transparent Pudding.

Melt half a pound of butter, and stir it into the same weight of double refined loaf sugar, add half a tea spoonful of essence of lemon, eight eggs, the whites and yolks beaten separately, and a couple of table spoonsful of cream. Set the whole on a few coals, stir it constantly till it thickens, take it off before it gets to boiling, and stir it till nearly cold, then turn it into a dish lined with pastry, put a rim of puff paste round the edge, and bake it half an hour. It will cut light and clear.

230. Lemon Syrup.

Mix a pint of lemon juice with a pound and three quarters of lump sugar. Dissolve it by a gentle heat, skim it until clear, then add one ounce of thin cut lemon peel, and simmer if gently for a few moments. Strain it through a flannel bag; when cold, bottle, cork, and seal it tight, keep it in a cool place. Another method of making it which is cheaper, and very good, is to dissolve half an ounce of citric acid, in a pint of clarified syrup, by a gentle heat; when cool, put in a few drops of oil or a little essence of lemon.

231. Orange Syrup.

Take nice fresh oranges, squeeze out the juice, and strain it; to a pint of juice put a pound and a half of while sugar. Dissolve it over a moderate fire, put in the peel of the oranges, and let the whole boil eight or ten minutes. Strain it till clear, through a flannel bag, bottle and cork it tight. This is nice to flavor puddings and pies, or sherbet.

232. Blackberry Syrup.

Pick over blackberries that are perfectly ripe, boil them in their juice till they break to pieces, then strain them through a flannel cloth, and to each pint of juice put a pound of sugar. Boil it again for ten minutes, then strain it and add a wine glass of brandy to each pint of syrup. When cool, bottle and cork it tight, and set it in a cool place. This mixed with cold water in the proportion of a wine glass of it to two thirds of a tumbler of water is a very agreeable summer beverage, it also possesses fine medicinal properties.

233. Clarified Syrup for Sweet Meats.

For most kinds of fruit, one pound of sugar, to one of the fruit, is sufficient to preserve them; some kinds of fruit will do with less. Put your sugar into your preserving kettle, and turn in as much cold water as you think will cover your fruit, when put in, add the white of an egg to every three pounds of sugar, then put it over a slow fire; when the sugar has dissolved, put it where it will boil, let it boil several minutes, then take it from the fire, and skim it till clear, put it back on the fire, when the scum rises again, take the kettle off and skim it again, this operation repeat till it is perfectly clear, then put in the fruit. If you have not syrup enough to cover the fruit, take the fruit out and put in more cold water, and let it get to boiling before you put in the fruit, if you have too much syrup, it should boil away before you boil your fruit in it. White sugar is better than brown for preserving, but brown sugar answers very well for common sweet meats. Every kind of ware but iron, will do to preserve in, but earthen ware is the best on account of its not imparting an unpleasant taste, to the sweet meats.

234. To Preserve Quinces.

Quinces if very ripe, are best pared and cut in slices about an inch thick, the cores should be taken out carefully with a small knife, then put the quinces in clarified syrup, and boil them till you can stick a broom splinter through them easily, take them up and put them in jars, and turn the syrup over them, cover them up, and put them in a cool place, as soon as done. Quinces preserved in this manner retain more of their natural flavor, but they cannot be preserved in this way without they are very ripe. If not very ripe pare and halve them, and take out the cores. Boil the quinces till tender, then take them out, strain the water they were boiled in, and use it to make a syrup for the quinces, allow a pound of sugar to a pound of the fruit, when clarified put in the quinces and boil them slowly half an hour. Set them away in jars covered with a paper wet in brandy. Look at them in the course of three or four days, and if they have begun to ferment, turn off the syrup, and scald it, then turn it back on the quinces. Some people boil the cores of the quinces with them, but the syrup does not look as nice for it. A cheap way of preserving quinces, which is very good for common use, is to boil the parings and cores in cider till tender, then strain the cider, and for ten pounds of quince, put in two pounds of brown sugar, and a couple of quarts of molasses, and the beaten whites of two eggs; put it on the fire, clarify it, then put in the quinces, which should be pared and halved, put in the peel of an orange, boil them till tender.

235. Quince Marmalade.

Wash and quarter them, put them on the fire, with a little water, and stew them till tender enough to rub through a sieve. When strained, put to a pound of pulp, a pound of brown sugar, set it back on the fire, and let it stew slowly, stir it constantly. To ascertain when it is done, take a little of it out and let it get cold, if it then cuts smooth and clear it is sufficiently stewed. Crab apple

marmalade, is made in the same
manner.

236. To Preserve Pears.

Take an ounce of race ginger, for
every pound of pears. Scrape off the
skin, cut it into thin slices, and boil it until
tender, then take it from the fire, put in
your sugar, allowing three quarters of a
pound to a pound of the pears, set it on
the fire, clarify it, then put in the pears, if
very small they are good preserved
whole, boil them till tender, then put
them in jars tightly covered, set them
away in a cool place. In the course of
five or six days, boil the syrup again, and
turn it on them while hot. Choke and
Vergoulouse are the best pears for
preserving. The ginger can be omitted if
not liked.

237. To Preserve Peaches.

Pare your peaches, which should be
very ripe, and if you wish to preserve
them whole, allow a pound of sugar, to a
pound of fruit. Take lump sugar, break it
into small pieces, and dip each piece
into cold water, let it be in just long
enough to get saturated with the water,
then put the lumps into a preserving
kettle, set the kettle over a slow fire,
when the sugar has dissolved, put in
your peaches, boil them twenty minutes.
These as well as all other sweet meats,
should be set away in a cool place, as
soon as done, if allowed to stand by the
fire for a few hours, the syrup will not
look clear; all preserves should be
covered up tight. Let them remain

several days, then turn the syrup from them, scald it, and turn it back on to them, while hot. If you preserve your peaches without the stones, three quarters of a pound of sugar to a pound of fruit is sufficient, take those that are mellow and juicy, pare and halve them, take out the stones, put them in a deep dish; on each layer of peach, sprinkle your sugar, let them stand three or four hours, then put them on the fire with very little water, let them boil slowly for twenty minutes.

238. To Preserve Currants.

Take your currants from the stems, for a pound of currants, allow a pound of sugar. Make some syrup, clarify it, and put in the currants, let them boil slowly for a few moments. A table spoonful of these, mixed with a tumbler of water is a very wholesome drink in the summer.

239. To Preserve Barberries.

Pick over your barberries, and put them in clarified syrup, boil them half an hour. Molasses does very well to preserve barberries in, for common use, with a little orange peel boiled with them. Preserved barberries mixed with water, is a very refreshing drink in fevers.

240. To Preserve Ginger.

Take green ginger, and soak it until you can scrape off the outside, when scraped, soak it in salt and water one day, then take it out of the salt and water, and boil it till tender. Make a syrup of white sugar, allowing equal weights of sugar and ginger, when clarified take it off, and when cold, turn it on the ginger, let it remain a week, then boil the ginger and syrup together, until the syrup appears to have entered the ginger, when cool put in a little essence of lemon.

241. To Preserve Apples.

Take nice tart apples, halve and quarter them, and take out the cores. For a pound of apples, allow three quarters of a pound of sugar. When you have clarified your syrup, put in the apples, with the skin of a lemon pared thin. When the apples are tender, take them up, and let the syrup remain till cold, then turn it over them. Apples preserved in this manner, will keep but a few days. Crab apples should be preserved whole, with the skins on, and to a pound of the apples put a pound of sugar.

242. To Preserve Cymbelines
or Mock Citron.

Cut and scrape the rinds of cymbelines, put them in strong salt and water, let them remain in it a week, then in fair water three days, changing the water every day, then soak them in alum water an hour. Tie up oyster shells, in a cloth, and boil them with the cymbelines. When the cymbelines are tender, take them up and put them in alum water. Make your syrup, allowing a pound and a half of sugar, to a pound of the melon, boil your cymbelines in it three quarters of an hour. These are good eaten as any other preserves, or put in cake instead of citron.

243. To Preserve Watermelon Rinds.

Take the rind of a nice watermelon, cut it in strips and boil them a quarter of an hour, with a tea spoonful of saleratus to three or four quarts of water, then soak them in alum water an hour, rinse and put them in clarified syrup, and boil them twenty minutes. When they have stood three or four days, turn the syrup from them, and boil it, then turn it back on the rinds while hot. Allow equal weights of rinds and sugar.

244. To Preserve Cherries.

Allow three quarters of a pound of sugar, to a pound of cherries. Make your syrup, allowing half a pint of water, to two pounds of cherries, put in your cherries, shake them occasionally to prevent their sticking to the kettle. When the syrup is colored strain the cherries.

245. To Preserve Muskmelons.

Procure muskmelons that are perfectly green, the later in the season, the better. Scrape off the skin of the rind, taking care not to scrape the green part. Cut them through the middle, and take out the seeds, then cut them in the form of rings an inch thick. Put them in salt and water, and let them lay several days, then in fair water one day, changing the water several times; take them out and soak them in alum water, one or two hours. Take race ginger, the green is the best, soak it until you can scrape off the outside, cut it in slices, and boil it until tender. Boil your melons in fresh water, with a handful of peach leaves, and the ginger, allowing half an ounce to each pound of fruit. When the melon is tender, put it in alum water, together with the ginger. Make the syrup for the melons, allowing a pound of white sugar, to a pound of the fruit, when clarified put in the melons, and boil them, together with the ginger, half an hour, take them up, turn the syrup over them, when cool, drop in a little essence of lemon.

When they have stood several days turn the syrup from them, boil and turn it back while hot, to the melons.

246. To Preserve Pine Apples.

Pare off the rind of the pine apples, cut them in slices an inch thick. Weigh out a pound of white sugar, allowing a pound of it to each pound of fruit, lay your pine apples in a deep dish, on each layer of it sprinkle some of your sugar, (which should be powdered.) Set the pine apples away till the next day, reserving part of the sugar. Then turn the syrup from the pine apples into your preserving pan, add your reserved sugar, put in a tea cup of water, to the juice of four or five pine apples, clarify it, then put in the apples, and boil them till tender. Let the whole stand in a dish several days, and if there is any appearance of fermentation, put it in a preserving pan, scald it through, then turn it into glasses, and set it in a cool place.

247. To Preserve Pumpkins.

Take a good sweet pumpkin, halve it, take out the seeds, and cut it in chips, of the size of a dollar. To each pound of pumpkin, allow a pound of powdered loaf sugar, and a gill of lemon juice. Put your pumpkin chips in a dish, and to each layer, put a layer of sugar, turn the lemon juice over the whole, and let it stand a day, then boil it till tender, with half a pint of water to four or five pounds of the pumpkin. Tie up ginger in a bag, and boil with it, also the rind of several lemons, cut into chips.

248. To Preserve Gages.

Take equal quantities of fruit and sugar. Make a syrup of the sugar, (which should be white,) with a little water, when it boils drop in the plums, boil them very slowly for a few moments, then take them up into dishes, and let them remain several days, then boil them again, until the syrup appears to have entered them. Put the plums in jars, boil the syrup again, in the course of two or three days, and turn it over them.

249. To Preserve Strawberries.

Take Chili or field strawberries, and hull them. Take equal quantities of fruit, and white sugar, and put a layer of each alternately in a preserving pan, having a layer of strawberries at the bottom, let them stand for half an hour, then put a gill of cold water with them, to prevent their burning at the bottom of the pan. Set them over a moderate fire, when the juice runs freely increase the fire, until they boil briskly, when they have boiled half an hour, take them up, turn them into bottles, cork them tight, and dip the mouths of the bottles into hot sealing wax. Keep them in dry sand.

250. Blackberry and Raspberry Jam.

For a pound of berries allow a pound of brown sugar, put a layer of each alternately in a dish, let them stand two or three hours, strain them, put them over a moderate fire, and boil them half an hour.

251. Strawberry, Blackberry, and Raspberry Jelly.

Pick over your fruit carefully, then mash and squeeze the berries through a flannel bag, to each pint of juice put a pound of white sugar, set it on the fire, when it has boiled seven or eight minutes, take it from the fire and skim it till clear, then put it back on the fire; as fast as the scum rises take it from the fire, and skim it. To ascertain when it is done, take a little of it from the fire, and let it be till cold.

252. Cranberry, Grape and Currant Jelly.

Wash and drain the berries till nearly dry, then put them in a preserving pan, with a plate at the bottom, heat them till they break, then strain them through a flannel cloth; to each pint put a pound of white sugar. Boil and skim them till perfectly clear, the kettle should be taken from the fire when skimmed. When the jelly has boiled four or five

hours, take a little of it up, and put it in a
tumbler of cold water, if it sinks to the
bottom in a solid mass, it is done
sufficiently. Jellies are improved, by
being put in the sun for several days.
Care must be taken, that the dew does
not fall on them.

Notes

253. Quince Jelly.

Halve your quinces, take out the
cores, and boil the quinces until very
soft, in just sufficient water to cover
them, then squeeze them through a
flannel bag, and to a pound of quince
pulp, put a pound of white sugar. Boil
and skim it till clear; when it becomes a
jelly, strain it again, fill your glasses and
cover them tight.

254. Apple Jelly.

Take greenings, pippins or crab
apples, halve them and take out the
cores, boil them till tender in water just
sufficient to cover them, boil with them
the peel and juice of a lemon, to every
three pounds of the apple. Strain the
apple, and to each pound, put a pound
of loaf sugar. Boil and skim it till clear;
when it becomes a jelly, take it up, color
it if you like, either with saffron, beet
juice, or cochineal. Strain it, and put it in
glasses, and set them in a cool place.

255. Lemon Jelly.

Put on a slow fire an ounce and a
half of isinglass, (pulled into small
pieces,) a pint of water, with the rind of
several lemons; when dissolved put in a
pint of lemon juice, a pound and a half of

white sugar, color it with a few grains of saffron, strain it through a flannel bag, then boil it ten or fifteen minutes, strain it till clear, let it remain till nearly congealed, then fill your glasses or moulds with it. To get it out of the moulds dip them into lukewarm water for a minute, the jelly will then come out easily.

256. Calf's Foot Jelly.

To four feet put four quarts of water, boil them till tender, and the water boils away to one quart. Take it off, let it stand till cold, then skim off the fat carefully, and put the jelly into a preserving pan, and set it on the fire; when it melts take it from the fire, put in the beaten whites of seven eggs, a little cinnamon, half a pint of white wine, the juice of two lemons, and the rind, leaving out the white part; sweeten the whole to your taste, with loaf sugar. Put it back on the fire, and boil it fifteen minutes, then strain it through a flannel bag, without squeezing it, if it is not clear the first time it is strained, strain it till it is. The bag should be suspended on a nail over a dish, and the jelly poured into it, and allowed to drain through it gradually. When clear turn it into cups or glasses, and set them where the jelly will congeal, but not so cold as to freeze it. This kind of jelly will not keep longer than two or three days in warm weather. A knuckle of veal makes a jelly as good as calves' feet, it is made in the same manner. Jellies and sweet meats are less liable to ferment, if kept in glass jars or bottles. A paper wet in spirits and put over sweet meats, has a tendency to prevent their fermenting. Sweet meats should be carefully watched during warm weather, and if fermentation commences turn the syrup from them, scald it, and turn it back.

257. Coffee.

To make good strong coffee, allow for each person a heaping table spoonful of ground coffee, and a pint of water. Put your coffee into a tin pot, with a piece of fish skin about the size of a ninepence, to two or three quarts of water, turn on your water boiling hot, and boil the coffee from fifteen to twenty minutes, take it off, and let it stand to settle five or six minutes, then turn it off carefully. French coffee is made in a German filter, the water is turned on to it boiling hot, an ounce to each person is allowed, put in a piece of fish skin before you turn on the water. When cream cannot be preserved for coffee, boiled milk is a good substitute. Many people dislike to settle coffee with fish skin, thinking it imparts a disagreeable taste to the coffee, but it is owing to its not being prepared properly, the skin should be taken from mild codfish, washed, and cut into small pieces and dried perfectly. The white of an egg, egg shells, and isinglass, are all good to settle coffee. The best kind of coffee is old Java, and Mocha; before it is roasted, it should be hung over the fire two or three hours to dry, if dried in the oven it looses its strength, it should be hung at such a distance from the fire, as to be in no danger of burning. When dry put it on hot coals, and stir it constantly till done, which is ascertained by biting one of the lightest kernels, if it is brittle, the whole is done. Put it in a box, and cover it up tight, to keep in the steam. Coffee is much better roasted in a coffee roaster, than a kettle, as the fine aromatic flavor of the coffee is preserved, which escapes in a great measure, when roasted in an open kettle.

258. To make Tea.

Scald your tea pot, and put in a tea spoonful of tea, for each person that is to drink it, if it is a weak kind of tea, more will be required, pour on just boiling water enough to cover it, let it stand six or eight minutes, not longer if you wish to have it in perfection, pour on the rest of the water boiling hot.

259. Chocolate.

Scrape the chocolate off fine, and mix it smoothly with a little cold milk, or water. If liked very rich, make it entirely of milk, if not, use equal quantities of milk and water, boil it, then stir in the chocolate while boiling, sweeten it to your taste, let it boil five or six minutes; if liked rich, grate in a little nutmeg. A heaping table spoonful of grated chocolate to a pint of milk, or water, is the right proportion.

260. Hop Beer.

For three gallons of beer, take nine quarts of water, six ounces of hops. Boil the hops in half the water three hours, strain it, then boil the hops again in the remainder of the water, three hours longer, with a tea cup of ginger. Strain and put it with the rest of the liquor, and two quarts of molasses, and when lukewarm, put in a pint of new yeast, without any salt in it. Keep it in a temperate place, till it has ceased fermenting, which is ascertained by the froth subsiding. Turn it off carefully into a cask, or bottle it; it should not be corked very tight, or it will burst the bottles. Keep the bottles in a cool place.

261. Spruce Beer.

Take five gallons of water, and boil with a couple of ounces of hops, when it has boiled four or five hours, strain it, put to it two quarts of molasses, when lukewarm, put in a pint of fresh yeast, without any salt in it, (brewer's is the best,) put in three table spoonsful of the essence of spruce. A decoction made of the leaves of white or black spruce, is equally as good as the essence; boil the hops with the leaves. Let the beer stand in a temperate situation, several days exposed to the air, then put it in a cask, or bottle it, it will be fit to drink in the course of a few days. This is a nice summer drink, and a powerful antiscorbutic.

262. Spring Beer.

Take a small bunch each of sarsaparilla, sweet fern, wintergreen, sassafras, and spice wood, boil them with three ounces of hops, to six gallons of water, pare two or three raw potatoes, and throw them into the beer while it is boiling. When it has boiled five or six hours, strain it, and put to it three pints of molasses, when cool stir in a pint of fresh yeast, if the beer is too thick, dilute it with a little cold water. When fermented, bottle and keep it in a cool place.

263. Ginger Beer.

Take three table spoonsful of ginger, one of cream of tartar, and boil them gently in a gallon of water, with a lemon cut in slices; sweeten it to your taste, with loaf or Havana sugar, boil it three quarters of an hour. Strain it, and when cool, put in a tea cup of yeast; as soon as it has ceased fermenting, bottle it.

264. A good Family Wine.

Take equal parts of red and white currants, grapes, raspberries and English cherries, bruise and mix them with soft water, in the proportion of four pounds of fruit, to one gallon of water, let the liquid remain for two or three hours, then strain it, and to each gallon of wine add three pounds of sugar. Let it stand open three days, stirring it frequently, skim, and put it in a cask, place it in a temperate situation, where it will ferment slowly, when fermented add to it a ninth part of brandy, and stop it up tight. In two or three years it will be very rich.

265. Currant Wine.

Strain the currants, which should be perfectly ripe, to each quart of juice, put two of water, and three pounds of sugar. Stir the whole well together, and let it stand twenty four hours, then skim it, and set it in a cool place, where it will ferment slowly, let it remain three or four days, if at the end of that time, it has fermented, add one quart of French brandy, to every fifteen gallons, stop it tight, when it is clear, it is fit to bottle. This wine is better for being kept several years.

266. Raspberry Shrub.

To a quart of vinegar, put three quarts of fresh ripe raspberries, let it stand a day, then strain it, and to each pint, put a pound of white sugar. Put it in a jar, and set it in a kettle of boiling water, boil it an hour, skim it till clear. When cool add a wine glass of wine, to each pint of shrub. A couple of table spoonsful of this, mixed with a tumbler of water, is a very wholesome and refreshing drink in fevers.

267. Noyeau.

To three pints of good French brandy, put four ounces of bitter almonds, or peach meats bruised, put in half an ounce of cinnamon, the same quantity of mace and amber, pounded fine, add a tea spoonful of cloves; let it stand for a fortnight, shaking it often, then add a quart of water, and a pound and a quarter of sugar, let it stand a week, shaking it each day, then strain it off for use.

268. Spring Fruit Sherbet.

Boil in a quart of water six or eight stalks of the rhubarb plant, with the peel of a lemon pared very thin, and the juice of it. When it has boiled eight, or ten minutes, take it, sweeten it to the taste with any kind of syrup you like, or honey, flavor it with rosewater, strain it, let it stand five or six hours, it will then be fit to drink. It is a fine thing to assuage thirst.

269. Grape Wine.

To every gallon of ripe grapes, put a gallon of soft water, bruise the grapes, and let them stand a week, without stirring, then draw off the liquor carefully; to each gallon, put three pounds of lump sugar, when fermented, put it in a cask, stop it up tight, in six months it will be fit to bottle.

270. Smallage Cordial.

Take the young sprouts of smallage, wash and drain them till perfectly dry. Cut them into small pieces, and put them in a bottle, with stoned raisins, a layer of each alternately; when the bottle is two thirds full, fill it up with good French brandy. Cork it up, let it stand four or five days, then pour in as much more brandy, as you can get in. It will be fit for use in the course of a few days.

Miscellaneous Receipts, and observations
useful to young housekeepers.

1. To make Essence of Lemon.

Take one drachm of the best oil of lemon, and two ounces of strong rectified spirit. Mix the spirit by degrees, with the oil. Another way to procure the essence of the peel, is to rub the peel with lumps of sugar, till the yellow part is all taken up. Scrape off the surface of the sugar, and press it down tight, in a preserving pot, and cover it tight; a little of this sugar gives a fine flavor to pies or cake. This mode of procuring the essence of the peel, is superior to any other, as the fine flavor of the peel is extracted without any alloy.

2. Essence of Ginger.

Put three ounces of fresh grated ginger, an ounce of thin cut lemon peel, into a quart of brandy, or proof spirit, bottle and cork it, let it stand for ten days, shaking it up each day, it will then be fit for use. A few drops of this, in a little water, or on a lump of sugar, answers all the purposes of ginger tea, and is much more convenient and palatable.

3. Rose Water.

Gather your roses on a dry day, when full blown, pick off the leaves, and to a peck of them, put a quart of water. Put them in a cold still, and put it over a slow fire, the slower they are distilled the better. When distilled put it in the bottles, let it stand a couple of days, then cork it tight.

4. Spice Brandy.

Into a large wide mouthed bottle, put French brandy, and fresh rose leaves, or lemon and orange peel. When this has stood a week, it is nice spice for pies, puddings and cake. Peach meats or almonds steeped in brandy are very good spice for custards.

5. Barley Water.

Take a couple of ounces of pearl barley, wash it in cold water, and put it into half a pint of boiling water, and let it boil four or five minutes, then turn off the water, and pour on two quarts of boiling water, strain it, and put to it two ounces of figs sliced, two of stoned raisins, half an ounce of liquorice cut into small bits, and bruised, boil it till reduced to a quart, and strain it. This is a very wholesome drink in fevers.

6. Water Gruel.

Mix a couple of table spoonsful of Indian meal, with one of flour and a little water, stir it into a pint of boiling water, let it boil six or eight minutes, then take it up put in a piece of butter of the size of a walnut, pepper and salt, to your taste, and nutmeg, or cinnamon if you like, turn it on to toasted bread or crackers. To convert this into caudle, add a little ale; wine or brandy, and loaf sugar.

7. Wine Whey.

Into a pint of milk while boiling, stir a couple of wine glasses of wine, let it boil for a moment, then take it off, when the curd has settled, turn off the whey, and sweeten it with loaf sugar. Where wine cannot be procured, cider, or half the quantity of vinegar, is a good substitute.

8. Stomachic Tincture.

Bruise an ounce and a half of Peruvian bark, and one of bitter dried orange peel. Steep it in brandy or proof spirit, for a fortnight, shaking it each day. Let it remain for a couple of days without shaking it, then decant the liquor. A tea spoonful of it in a wine glass of water, is a fine tonic.

9. Beef Tea.

Broil a pound of fresh beef ten minutes, take it up, pepper and salt it, cut it into small pieces, and turn a pint of boiling water on to it, let it steep in a warm place for half an hour, then strain it off, and it is fit to drink. This is a quick way of making it, but the best way is to cut beef into small bits, and fill a junk bottle with it, stop it up tight, and immerse it in a kettle of cold water, put it where it will boil four or five hours. This way is superior to the other, as the juices of the meat are obtained unmixed with water; a table spoonful of this is as nourishing as a cup full of that which is made by broiling.

10. Carrageen or Irish Moss.

American, or Irish Carrageen, is a very nutritious and light article of food for children, and invalids, and is a good thickener of milk and broths, and for blanc mange is equal to the most expensive ingredients, while the cost is very trifling. The following decoction for consumptive patients, is recommended. Steep half an ounce of the moss in cold water, for a few minutes, then take it out, boil it in a quart of milk until it attains the consistency of warm jelly, strain it, and sweeten it to the taste, with white sugar or honey, flavor it with whatever spice is most agreeable, if milk is disagreeable, water may be substituted. If a tea spoonful of the tincture of rhutany is mixed with a cup full of the decoction, a tone will be given to the stomach, at the same time that nourishment is conveyed to the system.

11. Moss Blanc Mange.

Steep half an ounce of Irish moss in a pint and a half of milk; when it becomes a thick jelly sweeten it with loaf sugar, and flavor it with white wine and cinnamon. To make orange, lemon or savory jellies, use a similar process, substituting water for milk. Jellies made of it, are more nourishing, than those made of sago, tapioca or arrow root.

12. Elderberry Syrup.

Wash and strain the berries, which should be perfectly ripe, to a pint of the juice put a pint of molasses. Boil it twenty minutes, stirring it constantly; then take it from the fire, and when cold add to each quart four table spoonsful of brandy; bottle and cork it. This is an excellent remedy for a tight cough.

13. New Bread and Cake from old and rusked bread.

Bread that is several days old, may be renewed by putting it into a steamer, and steaming it from half to three quarters of an hour, according to its size; the steamer should not be more than half full, otherwise the water will boil up on to the bread. When steamed, wrap it up loosely in a dry cloth, and let it remain till quite dry, it will then appear like bread just baked. If pieces of bread are put in the oven and dried, several hours after baking in it, they will keep good a long time. They are good as fresh bread for dressing to meat, and for puddings, if soaked soft in cold water. Rich cake with wine or brandy in it, will keep good several months in winter, if kept in a cool place. The day it is to be eaten, it should be put in a tin pan, and set in a bake pan that has a tea cup of water in it, when heated thoroughly through take it up.

14. To Preserve Cheese from Insects and Mould.

Cover the cheese while whole with a paste made of wheat flour, put a piece of paper or cloth over it, and cover it with the paste, keep it in a cool dry place. Cheese that has skippers in it, if kept till cold weather will be free from them. Cheese that is growing mouldy can be prevented from becoming any more so, by grating it fine and moistening it with wine, and covering it up in a jar. It is preferred by many people to that which is not grated.

15. To keep Vegetables and Herbs.

Succulent vegetables, are preserved best in a cool shady place that is damp. Turnips, potatoes, and similar vegetables should be protected from the air and frost, by being buried in earth; in very severe cold weather, they should be covered with a linen cloth. It is said that the dust of charcoal will keep potatoes from sprouting, if sprinkled over them.—Herbs should be gathered on a dry day, either just before or while in blossom; they should be tied in bundles and hung in a shady airy place, with the blossoms downwards. When perfectly dry, put away the medicinal ones in bundles; pick off the leaves of those that are to be used in cooking, pound and sift them, and keep them in bottles corked tight.

16. To preserve various kinds of Fruit over winter.

Apples can be kept till June, by taking only those that are perfectly sound, and wiping them dry, and putting them in barrels with a layer of bran to each layer of apples. Cover the barrel with a linen cloth to protect them from the frost. Mortar put on the top of the apples, is said to be an excellent thing to prevent their decaying, as it draws the air from them, which is the principal cause of decay; the mortar should not touch the apples. To preserve oranges and lemons for several months, take those that are perfectly fresh, and wrap each one by itself in soft paper, and put them in glass jars, or a very tight box, strew white sand thickly round each one and over the top. The sand should be previously perfectly dried in the oven, several hours after baking in it. Cover the fruit up tight, and keep it in a cool dry place, but not so cold as to freeze it. To preserve grapes gather them on a dry day, when not quite dead ripe; pick those off from the stem, that are not perfectly fair, lay them in a glass jar and on each layer sprinkle a layer of dry bran, taking care that none of the grapes touch each other, have a layer of bran on the top of them, and cork and seal them tight. A box will do to keep them in if covered with mortar. To restore them to their freshness when they are to be eaten, cut the ends of the stalks and immerse them in wine, let them remain in it for a few moments before they are to be eaten. Various kinds of green fruit, such as grapes, currants, gooseberries and plums, can be kept the year round by putting them in bottles, and setting them in an oven four or five hours after baking in it; let them remain in it till they begin to shrink, then cork and seal them tight, they will be fit for pies, whenever you wish to use them. Ripe blackberries, and whortleberries, dried perfectly in the sun, and tied up in bags so as to exclude the air, will keep good over the winter. Whenever you wish to use them for pies, pour on boiling water enough to cover them, and let them remain in it till they swell to nearly the original size, then drain off the water, and use them.

17. To extract essences from various kinds of flowers.

Procure a quantity of the petals of any kind of flowers that have an agreeable fragrance. Card thin layers of cotton, which dip into the finest Florence oil. Sprinkle a small quantity of salt on the flowers, and put a layer of them in a glass jar or wide mouthed bottle, with a layer of the cotton, put in a layer of each alternately until the jar is full, then cover the top up tight with a bladder. Place the vessel in a south window, exposed to the heat of the sun. In the course of a fortnight, a fragrant oil may be squeezed from the cotton, little inferior if rose leaves are made use of, to the imported otto of rose.

18. Indelible Ink for marking linen.

Dissolve a drachm of lunar caustic, in half an ounce of pure cold water. Dip whatever is to be marked in pearlash water, dry it perfectly, then rub it smooth with a silver spoon, (ironing it sets the pearlash water,) write on it, and place it in the sun, and let it remain until the name appears plain and black. Red ink for marking linen, is made by mixing and reducing to a fine powder, half an ounce of vermilion, a drachm of the salt of steel, and linseed oil enough to render it of the consistency of black durable ink.

19. Perfume Bags.

Rose leaves dried in the shade, and mixed with powdered cloves, cinnamon and mace, put in small bags and pressed, is a fine thing to keep in drawers of linen, to perfume them.

20. Lip Salve.

Dissolve a small lump of white sugar, in a table spoonful of rose water, clear water will do but is not as good. Mix it with a table spoonful of sweet oil, a piece of spermaceti of the size of half a butternut. Simmer the whole together about eight or ten minutes.

21. Bread Seals.

Take the crust of newly baked bread, moisten it with gum water and milk, add either vermilion in powder or rose pink, to color it. When moistened work it with the fingers till it forms a consistent paste without cracking; it should then be laid in a cellar, till the next day. Then break it into pieces of the size you wish to have the seals, warm and roll them into balls, press one at a time, on the warm impression of a seal press. The bread should go into every part of the sealing wax impression; while the bread remains on it, pinch the upper part so as to form a handle, to hold the bread seal when in use. Take off the bread seal, trim all the superfluous parts, put the seals where they will dry slowly. The more the bread has been worked with the fingers, the more glossy and smooth will be the seals, and the better impression will they make.

22. To loosen the Glass Stopples of Decanters or Smelling Bottles when wedged in tight.

Rub a drop or two of oil with a feather round the stopple, close to the mouth of the bottle or decanter, then place it between one and two feet from the fire. The heat will cause the oil to run down between the stopple and mouth. When warm strike it gently on both sides with any light wooden instrument, you may happen to have; then try to loosen it with the hand. If it will not move, repeat the process of rubbing oil on it, and warming it. By persevering in this method, you will at length succeed in loosening it, however firmly it may be wedged in.

23. Cement for broken China, Glass and Earthenware.

To half a pint of skimmed milk, add an equal quantity of vinegar to curdle it, then separate the curd from the whey, and mix the curd with the whites of five eggs, beat the whole well together, then add enough of the finest quicklime to form a consistent paste. (Plaster of Paris is still better if it can be procured, than lime.) Rub this mixture on the broken edges of the china or glass, match the pieces and bind them tightly together, and let them remain bound several weeks. They will then be as firm as if never broken. Boiling crockery in milk is a good thing to cement them, the pieces should be matched, bound with pieces of cloth, and boiled half an hour, they should remain in the milk till cold, and not be used for several weeks. Pulverized quicklime mixed with the white of an egg and rubbed in the cracks of china and glass, will prevent their coming apart; the dishes should be bound firmly for several weeks, after it is rubbed in. The Chinese method of mending broken china, is to grind flint glass, on a painter's stone, as fine as possible, and then beat it, with the white of an egg to a froth, and lay it on the edges of the broken pieces. It should remain bound several weeks. It is said, that no art will then be able to break it in the same place.

24. Japanese Cement or Rice Glue.

Mix rice flour intimately with cold water, and then gently boil it. It answers all the purposes of wheat flour paste, and is far superior in point of transparency and smoothness. This composition made with a comparatively small proportion of water, that it may have the consistence of plastic clay, will form models, busts, statues, basso relievos and similar articles. The Japanese make fish of it which very much resemble those made of mother of pearl. Articles made of it when dry are susceptible of a very high polish. Poland starch, is a very nice cement, for pasting layers of paper together, and any fancy articles when it is necessary.

25. Cement for Alabaster.

Take of bees' wax one pound, of rosin half a pound, and three quarters of a pound of alabaster. Melt the wax and rosin, then strew the alabaster, previously reduced to a fine powder, over in it lightly. Stir the whole well together, then knead the mass in water, in order to incorporate the powder thoroughly with the rosin and wax. Heat the cement and the alabaster, which should be perfectly dry, when applied join and keep it bound a week. This composition when properly managed forms an extremely strong cement.

26. To Extract Fruit Stains.

Hold the spot over steam till quite moist, then over burning sulphur; the sulphurous gas will cause the spot to disappear.

27. To extract spots of paint from Silk, Woolen and Cotton Goods.

Saturate the spots with spirits of turpentine, let it remain several hours, then take the cloth and rub it between the hands. It will crumble away and not injure either the texture or color of the cloth.

28. To remove black stains on Scarlet Merinos or Broadcloths.

Wash the stain in water with a little tartaric acid in it, rinse it directly, and care should be taken not to get any of the acid water on the clean part of the dress. Weak pearlash water is good to remove stains produced by acids.

29. To remove grease spots from Paper, Silk or Woolen.

Grate on chalk enough to cover the

grease spots. French chalk is the best, but common chalk will answer very well. Cover the spots with brown paper, and set a warm flat iron on the top, and let it remain until cold. Care must be taken not to get the iron so hot as to change the color of the article. If the grease does not appear to be extracted, on removing the flat iron, grate on more chalk, and heat the iron, and put it on again.

30. To extract stains from white Cotton goods and Colored Silks.

Spots of common or durable ink, can be removed by saturating them with lemon juice and salt in summer, and keeping them where the sun will shine on them several hours. Rub the juice and salt on them as fast as they get dry. Where lemons cannot be procured, tartaric acid dissolved in salt and water, is a good substitute. Iron mould can be removed in the same way; it is said that spirits of salts diluted with water will also extract iron mould. Sal ammoniac with lime, will take out the stains of wine. Mildew and most other stains on white goods, can be removed by rubbing on soft soap and salt, and putting them in a hot summer's sun, it should be rubbed on as fast as it dries. Where this fails, lemon juice and salt will be generally effectual. Colored cotton goods that have ink spilt on them, should be soaked in lukewarm milk or vinegar; sour milk is the best. Spirits of turpentine, alcohol or sal ammoniac, are all good to remove spots from colored silks.

31. Rules for washing Calicoes.

Calicoes that incline to fade, can have the colors set by washing them with beef's gall in clear water previous to washing them in soap suds; a small tea cup full to a pail of water is the right proportion. By squeezing out the gall, and bottling and corking it up, it can be kept several months. A little vinegar in the rinsing water of calicoes, that have green, pink or red colors, will brighten them and prevent their mixing together. Yellow calicoes should be washed in soap suds and not rinsed. A little salt in the rinsing water of calicoes, particularly blues and greens, tends to prevent their fading by subsequent washing, it will also prevent their catching fire readily. Thin starch water is good to wash fading calicoes in, but it is rather hard to get them clean in it; no soap is necessary. Calicoes should not be washed in very hot suds and soft soap should never be used, excepting for buff and yellows, for which it is the best. The two latter colors should not be rinsed in clear water.

32. Rules for washing Silks.

The water in which pared potatoes has been boiled, is an excellent thing to wash black silk in, it makes it look almost as black and glossy as new. Beef's gall in soap suds is also very good, and soap suds without the gall does very well. Colored silks should have all the spots removed before the whole of the article is wet. Put soap into boiling water and beat it till it is all dissolved, and forms a strong lather when at a hand heat, put in the article that is to be washed and if strong it may be rubbed hard; when clean squeeze out the water without wringing, and rinse it in warm water. Rinse it in another water and for bright yellows, crimsons, maroons and scarlets, put in oil of vitriol, sufficient to give the water an acid taste, for oranges, fawns, browns or their shades use no acids, for pinks, rose colors, and their shades, use tartaric acid, lemon juice or vinegar. For bright scarlet, use a solution of tin. For blues, purples, and their shades, add a small quantity of American pearlash, to restore the colors. Verdigris dissolved in the rinsing water of olive greens is good to revive the colors, a solution of copper is also good. Dip the silks up and down in the rinsing water, and take them out without wringing, and before they get perfectly dry fold them up tight and let them lay a few moments, then mangle them, if you have not a mangler, iron them on the wrong side. A little isinglass, dissolved in the rinsing water of blondes and gauzes, is good to stiffen them.

33. Rules for washing Woolens.

If you do not wish flannels to shrink, wash them in two good suds, made of hard soap, then wring them out, and pour boiling water on them, and let them remain in it till cold. A little indigo in the rinsing water of white flannels makes them look nicer. If you wish to shrink your flannels, wash them in suds made of soft soap, and rinse them in cold water. Colored woolens that incline to fade, should be washed with a little beef's gall in the suds. Cloth pantaloons look well washed with beef's gall in the suds; they should be pressed, when quite damp, on the wrong side.

34. Rules for washing white Cotton Clothes.

Table cloths that have coffee or any other stains on them, should have boiling water turned on them and remain in it till cold. The spots should be rubbed out before they are put in soap suds, or they will be set, so that they cannot be removed by subsequent washing. If a little starch is put in the rinsing water, the stains will come out more easily the next time they are washed. Any white cloths, that have fruit stains on them, should be washed in the same manner. It is a good plan, to soap and soak very dirty clothes over night; put them in when the water is lukewarm, and let them heat gradually, if they get to boiling it will not do any harm. Where rain water cannot be procured to wash with, a little lye in the proportion of half a pailful to seven or eight pails of hard water will soften it so that much less soap will be necessary. It is said that white clothes washed in the following manner will not need any rubbing. To five gallons of soft water, add half a gallon of lime water, a pint and a half of soap and a couple of ounces of the salts of soda. Wet the clothes thoroughly and soak the parts that are most soiled; if very dirty, they should be soaked over night. Heat the above mixture boiling hot, then put in the clothes, let them boil an hour, then drain and rinse them thoroughly in warm water, then in indigo water, and they are fit for drying. The soda can be procured cheap, by purchasing it in large quantities. It is a good plan to save the dirty suds after washing, to water your garden if you have one, it is also good to harden sandy cellars and yards.

35. To clean Silk and Woolen Shawls.

Pare and grate raw potatoes, put a pint of it in two quarts of clear water. Let it stand for five hours, then strain the water and rub through as much of the potatoe as possible; let it remain until perfectly clear, then turn off the water carefully. Put a clean white cloth on a table, lay the shawl on it and pin it down tight. Dip a clean sponge into the potatoe water and rub the shawl with it till clean, then rinse the shawl in clear water. When nearly dry, mangle it; if you have not a mangler, wrap it up in a clean white cloth and press it under a heavy weight till perfectly dry. All the grease spots and stains should be taken out of the shawls, before they are washed with the potatoe water.

36. To clean Silk Stockings.

Wash the stockings in mildly warm hard soap suds, rinse them in soap suds and if you wish to have them of a flesh color, put in a little rose, pink or cochineal powder; if you prefer a bluish cast, put in a little indigo. Hang them up to dry without wringing, when nearly dry, iron them on the right side, till perfectly so. If you wish silks of any kind to have a gloss on them, never rinse them without soap in the water.

37. To clean Carpets.

Carpets should be taken up as often as once a year, even if not much used, as there is danger of their getting moth eaten. If used much they should be taken up two or three times a year. If there is any appearance of moths when carpets are taken up, sprinkle a little black pepper or tobacco on the floor before the carpets are put down. Shake the dust out of the carpets, and if they are so much soiled as to require cleaning, rub a little dry magnesia or grated raw potatoes on them; the potatoes should be rubbed on with a new broom. Let it remain until perfectly dry before walking on it. If there are any grease or oil spots on the carpet, they should be extracted before the potatoe is rubbed on. They can be extracted by grating on potter's clay, covering it with brown paper and a moderately warm flat iron or warming pan. It will be necessary to do it several times to get out the whole of the grease.

38. To clean Feather Beds and Mattresses.

When feather beds become soiled or heavy, rub them over with a brush dipped into hot suds. When clean lay them on a shed or railing, where the rain will fall on them till they get thoroughly soaked, let them dry in a hot sun for a week, shaking and turning them over each day. This way of washing the beds makes the feathers fresh and light, and is much easier than the old fashioned way of emptying the beds, and washing the ticking and feathers separately, while it answers quite as well. Hair mattresses that have become hard and dirty, can be made nearly as good as new ones, by ripping them and washing the ticking, picking the hair free from bunches, and keeping it in an airy place several days. When the ticking gets dry fill it lightly, and tack it together.

39. To clean Light Kid Gloves.

Magnesia, moist bread and India Rubber, are all of them good to clean light kid gloves, if rubbed on thoroughly.

40. To remove Ink or Grease spots from Floors.

Ink spots can be removed by scouring them with sand, wet with water that has a few drops of oil of vitriol in it. Great care is necessary in using it, as it eats holes if suffered to remain long without having something put on to counteract its effects. When rubbed on floors, it should be rinsed off immediately with weak pearlash water. Oil and grease spots can be removed by grating on potter's clay thick and wetting it, it should remain on till it has absorbed all the grease; if brown paper and a warm iron is put on, it will come out much quicker. Pearlash water and sand is also good to extract grease and oil, they should be rubbed hard, then rinsed directly.

41. To clean Mahogany and Marble Furniture.

They should be washed in water without any soap. A little oil rubbed on them occasionally gives them a fine polish. White spots on varnished furniture can be removed by rubbing them with a warm flannel cloth dipped in spirits of turpentine. It is said that ink spots can be extracted by rubbing them with blotting paper rolled up tight.

42. To clean Stone Hearths and Stoves.

If you wish to preserve the original color of free stone hearths, wash them in clear water, then rub them with a stone of the same kind pounded fine, let it remain until dry, then rub it off. If the hearths are stained, rub them hard with a free stone. Hot soft soap or soap suds, does very well to wash hearths in, provided you have no objections to their looking dark. For brick hearths use redding mixed with thin starch and milk. Varnished stoves should have several coats of varnish put on in summer so as to get quite hard before being used. They should be washed in warm water without any soap, a little oil rubbed on once or twice a week, improves the looks of them. Black lead is good to black stoves that have never been varnished, but it will not do where they have been. It should be rubbed on dry once or twice a day.

43. To clean Brass.

Rotten stone and spirit, is better than any thing else to clean brasses with. Acids make them look nice at first, but they will not remain clean long, they are also apt to spot without a great deal of care is used. When brass andirons are not in use, they should be thoroughly cleaned with rotten stone, and rubbed over with oil, and wrapped up tight.

44. To cleanse Vials and Pie Plates.

Bottles and vials, that have had medicine in them, can be cleaned, by putting a tea spoonful or two of ashes in them and immersing them in cold water, the water should then be heated gradually until it boils. When they have boiled about half an hour, take them from the fire, and let them cool gradually in the water. Pie plates that have been baked on many times, are apt to impart an unpleasant taste to pies. It may be remedied by boiling them in ashes and water.

45. Cautions relative to
Brass and Copper.

Cleanliness has been aptly styled the cardinal virtue of cooks; food is not only more palatable cooked in a cleanly manner, but it is also more healthy. Many lives have been lost in consequence of carelessness in using copper, brass and glazed earthen utensils. No oily or acid substance should be allowed to cool or stand in them. Brass and copper utensils should be thoroughly cleaned with salt and hot vinegar before being used.

46. To keep Pickles and Sweet Meats.

Pickles should be kept in kegs or unglazed earthen jars. Sweetmeats keep best in glass jars, unglazed earthen jars do very well. If the jar is covered with a paper wet in spirits, the sweet meats are less liable to ferment. Both pickles and sweet meats, should be looked to occasionally to see that they are not fermenting, if so, the vinegar or syrup should be turned from them and scalded. If pickles grow soft, it is owing to the vinegar's not being strong enough; to make it stronger, scald it and put in a paper wet with molasses, and a little alum.

47. Starch.

To make good flour starch, mix the flour with a little water till free from lumps, thin it gradually with more water, then stir it slowly into boiling water. Let it boil five or six minutes stirring it frequently, a tallow candle stirred round in it several times makes it smoother. Strain it through a thick bag. Starch made in this manner will be free from lumps, and answers for cotton and linen as well as Poland starch. Many people like it for muslins. Poland starch is made in the same manner as flour starch. When rice is boiled in a pot without a bag, the water that it is boiled in is as good as Poland starch for clearing muslins, if boiled by itself a few moments and strained. Muslins to look very clear, should be starched and clapped while the starch is hot.

48. To temper New Ovens and Iron Ware.

New ovens before being used, to retain their heat well, should be heated half a day. The lid should be put up as soon as the wood is taken out. It should not be used to bake in the first time it is heated. Iron utensils are less liable to crack if heated gradually before they are used. New flat irons should be heated half a day, to retain their heat well.

49. To temper Earthen Ware.

Earthen ware that is used to cook in, is less liable to crack from the heat, by being put before they are used into cold water and heated gradually till the water boils, then taken from the fire and left in the water until cold.

50. Preservatives against the Ravages of Moths.

To prevent woolen and fur articles of dress, from getting moth eaten when you have done wearing them, put them in a chest with cedar chips, camphor gum or tobacco leaves.

51. To drive away various kinds of Household Vermin.

A little quicksilver and white of an egg beat together and put in the crevices of bedsteads, with a feather, is the most effectual bed bug poison. A solution of vitriol is also a good thing rubbed on walls that are infested by them. Hellebore with molasses rubbed on it, is an excellent thing to kill cockroaches, and put round the places that they are in the habit of frequenting. Arsenic spread on bread and butter, and placed round in rat holes, will put a stop to their ravages very speedily. Great care is necessary in using all these poisons where there are children, as they are equally as fatal to human beings as vermin. The flower of sulphur sprinkled round places that ants frequent, will drive them away. Half a tea spoonful of black pepper, one of sugar and a table spoonful of cream mixed and kept on a plate, in a room where flies are troublesome will soon cause them to disappear. Weak brine will kill worms in gravel walks. They should be kept moist with it a week, in the spring, and three or four days in the fall.

52. *To keep Meat in hot Weather.*
Cover it with bran, and keep it where there is a free circulation of air, away from the flies. A wire safe is an excellent thing to preserve meat from spoiling.

53. *To Prevent polished*
Cutlery from rusting.
Knives, snuffers and other steel articles, are apt to rust when not cleaned frequently. To prevent it wrap them tight in coarse brown paper, when not in use. Knives and forks should be perfectly free from spots and well polished when not in use. They should also be wrapped up, each one by itself, so as to exclude the air.

54. *To melt Fat for Shortening.*
The fat of all kinds of meat, excepting

mutton and hams, makes good shortening. Roast meat drippings and the liquor that meat is boiled in, should stand until cold to have the fat harden so that it can be taken off easily. Cut your scraps of fat into small pieces, and melt them slowly without burning, together with the fat from your drippings. When melted, strain it and let it remain until nearly cold, then pour in a little cold water. When the fat forms into a hard cake, take it up and scrape off the sediment that adheres to the under side, melt it again and when lukewarm sprinkle in a little salt. The dregs of fat are good for soap grease. This shortening answers all the various purposes of lard very well, excepting in the warmest weather. In using it for pies it is necessary to use considerable butter with it. The fat of meat should not be suffered to lie more than a week in winter without melting, and in summer not more than two or three days. Mutton fat and the fat of beef, if melted into hard cakes, will fetch a good price at the tallow chandler's. It is much more economical for housekeepers to put down their own pork, than to buy it already salted. The leaves and thin pieces that are not good for salting, should be cut into small bits and melted, then strained through a cullender with a cloth laid in it, as soon as it begins to thicken sprinkle in a tea cup of salt, to twenty or thirty weight of the lard; stir it in well, then set it away in a cool place. Some people have an idea that pork scraps must be fried till very brown in

order to be preserved good the year
round, but it is not necessary if salt is put
in.

55. *To preserve Eggs fresh a Year.*

Mix a handful of unslacked lime with
the same quantity of salt, two or three
gallons of water. If eggs that are
perfectly fresh are put in this mixture,
they will keep good a year in it, provided
none are cracked.

56. *To preserve Cream*
for long Voyages.

Take cream that is fresh and rich,
and mix it with half its weight of
powdered white sugar, stir the whole
well together, and preserve it in bottles
corked very tight. In this state it is ready
to mix with tea and coffee.

57. *Substitute for Milk and*
Cream in Tea or Coffee.

Beat the white of a fresh egg in a
bowl, and turn on to it gradually boiling
tea or coffee. It is difficult to distinguish
the taste from rich cream.

58. *To Cure Butter.*

Take two parts of the best common
salt, one part of sugar and one of
saltpetre, blend the whole well together.
Mix one ounce of this composition well
with every sixteen ounces of the butter.
Close it up tight in kegs, cover it with an
oiled paper, and let it remain untouched
for a month. Butter cured in this manner
is very nice, and will keep good eight or
nine months, if not exposed to the air.

59. To make salt Butter Fresh.

Put four pounds of salt butter into a churn, with four quarts of new milk and a small portion of annatto. Churn them together, take out the butter in the course of an hour, and treat it like fresh butter, working in the usual quantity of salt; a little white sugar improves it. This is said to be equal to fresh butter in every respect. The salt may be got out of a small quantity at a time, by working it over in fresh water, changing the water several times.

60. To take Rankness from a small quantity of Butter.

Take a quantity that is to be made use of, put it into a bowl filled with boiling water with a little saleratus in it, let it remain until cold, then take it off carefully and work it over with a little salt. By this method it is separated from the grosser particles.

61. Windsor Soap.

To make this celebrated soap for shaving and washing the hands, nothing more is necessary than to slice the best white soap as thin as possible and melt it over a slow fire. When melted take it up, when lukewarm scent it with the oil of caraway or any other oil that is more agreeable, then turn it into moulds and let it remain in a dry situation several days. It will then be fit for use.

62. To make Bayberry or Myrtle Soap.

To a pound of bayberry tallow, put a pint of potash lye, strong enough to bear up an egg. Boil them together till it becomes soap. Then put in half a tea cup of cold water, let it boil several minutes longer. Take it off, and when partly cooled put in a few drops of the essence of wintergreen, pour it into moulds and let it remain several days. This soap is good for shaving, and is an excellent thing for chapped hands and eruptions on the face.

63. Cold Soap.

To twenty pounds of white potash put ten of grease, previously melted and strained. Mix it well together with a pailful of cold water, let it remain several days, then stir in several more pailsful of cold water. Continue to pour in cold water at intervals of two or three days, stirring it up well each time. As soon as the water begins to thin it, it is time to leave off adding it. This method of making soap is much easier than any other, while it is equally cheap and good. If you have not land to enrich with your ashes they can be disposed of to advantage at the soap boiler's.

THE END.

Notes

Notes

Notes

Notes